Western Canadian Dictionary and Phrase Book

Facsimile of the 1913 edition
with an Introduction by John Orrell

The University of Alberta Press 1977

First published by
John Sandilands in 1912,
Second edition 1913

This facsimile of the 1913 edition
published by **The University of Alberta Press**
Edmonton, Alberta, Canada, 1977

Canadian Shared Cataloguing in Publication Data

Main entry under author

John Sandilands
Western Canadian Dictionary and Phrase Book.

ISBN 0 - 88864 - 021 - 8

1. English Language-Provincialisms
2. Canada-English Language-Slang
3. Canadianisms (English) 4. I Title

Pe 3237.S 3 1977
427′. 9′ 71
C.77 002209 X

Printed in Canada by
Printing Services of the University of Alberta

Introduction

Everybody has a vested interest in the language: in his own language first, and then, if he is privileged to know them, in those of other nations. We who call ourselves English-speaking Canadians have for the most part thought of our language as either <u>English or American</u>, for we call it the one and speak it with many of the inflexions of the other, recognizing our separateness from England but acknowledging too the very obvious fact that the words and the forms of our speech descend from those of the English people (or, more accurately, the British) and carry within them the rhythms of <u>Chaucer and Spenser and Shakespeare and Milton</u>.

John Sandilands' little dictionary has to do with the awkwardness and the excitement of that recognition, with all its ambiguities, paradoxes, and scope for irony. He published it first in 1912 in a staid and sober version, aiming simply to be helpful. It was, he claimed, the first dictionary ever printed in Canada, "Explaining in Plain English, for the Special Benefit of Newcomers, the Meaning of the Most Common Canadianisms and Colloquialisms." There may be other contenders for the prize of being first, but one could hardly doubt the authenticity of Sandilands' claim to be useful. He intends, he says, to include all the most common terms of trade and business that would "be unknown in the Old Country and in old lands, expressions which the newcomer is up against the moment he lands in the Dominion, and which heretofore he could only fathom by much questioning and consequent betrayal of the fact that he had just blown in."

Now although the first edition of the *Dictionary* was a relatively humourless affair, there is about the sentence I have just quoted a certain uneasy jocularity that betrays what I take to be John Sandilands' emerging recognition that what he had undertaken to do was impossible, and more than that, undesirable. Only a *very* pompous immigrant or a man in a funny story would actually question and betray in quite the way Sandilands imagines. In real life we pick up our language more subtly than that, and do our questioning and betraying by inference, punctuating our discoveries with hesitations, quick rushes of words, and a lot of listening.

So it is not surprising that the second edition of the *Dictionary*, which we reproduce here, has moved away from these unrealistic aims. What the editor gives us this time retains all the mechanics of lexicography that were found in the first, but they are transformed by a new sort of enthusiasm. For this second edition of 1913 is no mere utilitarian wordlist but a celebration of the rhythms and emphases of Canadian English. In entry after entry it exercises the reader in those forms of the language that distinguish it from its staider parent, and it need disturb no one that in doing so it is often a touch self-conscious, at times a touch vulgar. Look at the article under "Boost" and you will be reminded that 1913 was a boom year in the West, with visionary buildings springing almost ready-made, it seemed, out of the unresisting clay. The Great War and another kind of clay were yet to come, their threat as yet unfelt. Then Canadians would listen again to the plangent rhythms of Blighty; for the moment what mattered was the glad confidence of their own absorbing world and the pleasure of molding a new language in it.

It is doubtful, therefore, whether the *Dictionary* was ever much practical use to English-speaking immigrants, as a French or Italian phrase-book might be in Europe. Instead one can feel running through it a simple delight in being not-English, not-Blighty, not-Old-Country (see, for example, "All aboard!"), yet always Sandilands has his eyes peeled for Aunty on the other side of the Atlantic: "Interesting Souvenir to Send to Friends in the Old Country," he announces on the title-page of the first edition, and the second closes with a similar note.

A celebration, then, and not a technical book. The best way to read it is to take pot luck and see what you come across. The next best way is to use Sandilands' contents page, where you will find directions to some of the more amusing entries.

My thanks are due to the Emil Skarin Memorial Fund Committee, without whose generous support this little book could not have been republished. And all our thanks are due to John Sandilands, whose only memorial, it seems, rests in the pages of his *Dictionary*. But who could ask for more? *Si monumentum requiris, circumspice.*

John Orrell
September 1977

Western Canadian Dictionary and Phrase=Book

Things a Newcomer Wants to Know

WORDS THAT ARE DIFFERENT

Where they are not different, the meaning here attached is that which
is accentuated in Canada. Where, however, both words
and meaning are alike, "there's a reason"
for their inclusion

EDITED AND PUBLISHED BY JOHN SANDILANDS

FIRST DICTIONARY
EVER PRINTED
IN CANADA

Printed by
Telegram Job Printers Limited, 56 Adelaide Street
Winnipeg, Canada

SOME CONTENTS

After-thoughts. *That this edition can stand without a preface; that an early reprint will provide an opportunity for further embellishments and additions; and that suggestions, contributions and advertisements should be sent in without loss of time, addressed to John Sandilands, Western Canadian Dictionary, 56 Adelaide Street, Winnipeg, Man.*

Western Canadian Dictionary and Phrase=Book

Acadia, the name given to Nova Scotia and New Brunswick by the French, who were the earliest settlers there.

Acclamation. A candidate who is unanimously elected to office without the trouble of going to the poll is said to be elected by acclamation.

Acclimated, acclimatised; a word that, contracted in error, has now passed into currency.

Accommodations. Frequently this word takes the plural form, but correct writers do not use the final "s."

According to Hoyle, quite accurate, strictly in order, or according to the letter of the law; Hoyle being an authority on card games. If a person's action is questioned, he may protest that it is **according to Hoyle.**

Accountant, a bookkeeper, a clerk. Note that the word clerk, in Canada and the States, is generally used in reference to a shop assistant or counter-man.

Adanac, the word Canada spelt the reverse way, and frequently used as a name for hotels, clubs, and special brands of manufactured articles.

Agent, the railway official in charge of the smaller stations. As the town develops, the **agent** develops into a **stationmaster.** The word **agent** has all the other meanings which are attached to it in the Old-Country, but with this word, as with many other words here included, which are common in both Great Britain and Canada, we here give only the meaning which is new or accentuated in Canada.

Aim to please, a phrase borrowed from the language of the gun-men, who would **aim to kill.** The up-to-date and facetious entertainer or storekeeper now frequently advertises that he **aims to please.**

Air line, a straight line to a given point, a bee line. (See **Bee line**).

Alberta, the most western Prairie Province, with Saskatchewan on the east and the Rocky Mountains and British Columbia on the west. Edmonton is its capital, and, after that,
its most important city is Calgary. (See **Foothills.**)

Alfalfa, the common name of lucerne, a valuable, clover-like forage grass.

Alienation has all the meanings attached to the word in the **Old-Country,** but in Canada and the States prominence is given to the fact that it also means **mental derangement.**

Alienism, the study and treatment of mental derangements.

Alienist, a physician who has made a special study of diseases of the brain and nervous system, and is considered an expert.

All aboard! the train conductor's call to passengers when the train is about to pull out. At such a moment in the Old Country, the railway officials smilingly invite the first-class passengers and deadheads to "take your seats, gentlemen, please," and bang the doors on the third-class passengers' fingers.

All-fired, a general intensive, as **all-fired abuse; all-fired racket,** a great noise or disturbance; **all-fired hurry,** a tremendous hurry.

All in, in lots of trouble, played his last card, no resources left.

All kinds of work for you to do really means "Any amount of work waiting for you," and not various kinds of work as the Canadian expression would suggest to the new-comer.

All right, all right, is how an assertion is often wound up, as "I think I can hold down this job all right, all right," "I've just had a bully good dinner all right, all right," etc.

Almighty dollar, an American expression indicating the manner in which money is worshipped.

All wool and a yard wide, a metaphor implying that an article is of first-class quality and ample measure. Sometimes, also, it is applied to individuals of exceptional ability or sterling character.

America, the United States.

American (n.), a native of the United States. **American** (adj.), something pertaining to the United States.

Americanism, a phrase or word peculiar to the United States.

(3)

American plan. These words may be seen posted up in certain hotels, notifying that all guests are charged a flat rate per day for bedroom accommodation and the regular number of meals, in contradistinction to the **European plan,** which charges for bedroom and just the meals ordered or eaten.

Andirons, fire-dogs, the horizontal metal standards which support the logs in an open fireplace.

Antagonise, to contend, to strive; usually, however, used in a negative sense, as "We do not wish to **antagonise** the company," We do not wish to turn the company into antagonists.

Ante, a player's contribution to the poker game, or the stake. **Raise the ante,** to increase the stake.

Any old time is how the Canadian will refer to any indefinite period of chance or fate; **any old time** being the time when the expected or unexpected may happen. The signs of the times make it apparent that the new baby may arrive at **any old time,** or someone's illness has taken a turn for the worse and he may "drop off" **at any old time,** or a couple may be head and ears in love with each other and may now get married at **any old time. Any old time** is just any time at all, and the inference is that it is nearer than you might expect.

Apartment block, a residential block divided up into perfectly self-contained suites, somewhat after the style of the houses of flats in Scotland and in London, England.

Appropriation, a sum of money allotted by the Dominion Parliament, a Provincial Legislature, or a civic authority for a department or for some special purpose. In Old-Country governmental or civic circles it would be described as a vote.

Army. (See **Militia**).

Around, about. **Around one o'clock,** somewhere about one o'clock, before or after. **Around Winnipeg,** in or about Winnipeg.

Asleep at the switch, a metaphor implying unwatchfulness or asleep on duty. (See **Switchman**).

Assembler, an engineer, or machinist, who assembles, or arranges, the parts of a machine previous to erecting.

Assignment, an engagement, or a duty which has been asigned to a certain person. Thus the "engagement book" found in the reporters' rooms of Old-Country newspapers, where coming events are noted, and the name of a reporter placed opposite on the eve of the event, becomes the **assignment book** in the newspaper offices of the West.

Assiniboia, the name given to the colony which grew out of the Red River Settlement and which was changed to Manitoba when formed into a Province in 1870.

Atlantic Ocean is referred to as the **Herring Pond,** the **Puddle,** the **Big Drink,** etc.

A to Zee, from beginning to end. The confident applicant for a position, if asked if he is competent, may reply that he knows the whole business from **A to Zee.**

Aurora borealis, northern lights; a phenomenal kind of illumination in the northern part of the heavens, supposed to be due to electro-magnetic influences in the rare upper atmosphere. It occurs at various times, by night and day, and is usually characterized by the appearance of ribbon-like streams of light radiating from the region of the magnetic pole and extending toward the zenith. These phenomena constantly shift their positions and assume a variety of charming colours. Seen in the Old-Country, but more frequently in Canada.

B

Babbitt, a mixture of copper and tin used to prevent friction on machine bearings.

Back east. (See **Down east**).

Back number, a person who, like a back number of a magazine or periodical, has had his day and is no longer in demand.

Back-set. The prairie is first "broken"; that is, ploughed as thin as possible, and **back-setting** is a second and deeper ploughing, after the original surface sod has rotted.

Backwoods, a word now only found in old romances and early settlers' letters. The backwoods are now known as the bush, forest fires and the axe of the lumberjack having denuded the land of much of its forest wealth.

Bad. (See **In bad**).

Badger, an immigrant from Wisconsin, a State where badgers once abounded.

Bad man, a colloquialism meaning that the person is a hold-up or a desperado, such a man as really tries to be bad. "A professional fighter or man-killer, but who is sometimes perfectly honest. These men do most of the killing in frontier communities; yet the men who are killed generally deserve their fate. They are used to brawling, are sure shots, and able to draw their weapon with marvellous quickness. They think nothing of murder, are the terror of their associates, yet are very chary of taking the life of a man of good standing, and will often weaken, and back down, at once if confronted fearlessly. Stockmen have united to put down these dangerous characters, and many localities once infested by bad men are now perfectly law-abiding " (Roosevelt).

Baggage, luggage or portable property belonging to a passenger. **Baggage-master,** the train official who has charge of the luggage, or

baggage. **Baggage-check,** a baggage or cloak-room check. **Baggage-room,** where passengers' baggage is temporarily deposited.

Baggage transfer and express, the business of conveying luggage and parcels; though, where the sign "Baggage Transfer and Express" hangs out, one may obtain a rig for almost any purpose. (See **Rig**).

Bagman, a commercial traveller or drummer. (See **Drummer**).

Baled hay, tobacco or cigars with which a smoker has become dissatisfied, or the trash that "the other fellow" smokes. The ungrateful borrower who wishes to cast aspersions on the contents of your pouch may also remark on its resemblance to **baled hay.**

Balled-up, tangled, mixed up. A person may be **all balled-up** in his accounts, in his work, or in telling a story.

Band-saw, a continuous saw made in a strip which runs over pulleys in the same fashion as belting does. Band saws are now used in all modern lumber mills in preference to circular saws.

Band wagon, the allegorical vehicle which is conveying the leaders or the lusty enthusiasts in some popular movement or enterprise. The invitation to **get on the band wagon** may be construed as an appeal to hustle in and help, and share in the first fruits of victory.

Banner year, the best year, for crops, finance, building and progress generally. According to the Canadian booster, every year is a banner year, and with some truth, because Canada is an ever-growing country, with each year better than the last. **Best year ever** is another fashion of describing it.

Barker, a doorman who bawls out the attractions inside—in a show, a store, or elsewhere.

Barking up the wrong tree, falsely accusing, or accusing the wrong person. To get at the intended meaning of the phrase, one can imagine a dog barking up another tree than the one on which its prey escaped. Squirrels, coons, etc., run up a tree when chased by a dog; they pass from one tree to another in the branches until they are quite a distance from the tree they first ran up, the one the dog continues to bark up. He is **barking up the wrong tree.**

Barn, the stable for horses or cattle. The general storehouse on a farm. The covered sheds in which the street-cars are sheltered overnight are also called barns.

Barn boss, the man in charge of the barn (or stables) in a lumber camp, on a large farm, in a livery, or wherever a large number of horses are kept. (See **Livery**).

Barn-stormers, theatrical performers who range the country and do their stunts in barns, usually presenting lurid-coloured plays to suit an audience that is not over-critical.

Barred. When the edict has gone forth that a certain man cannot be again employed in an establishment he is said to be **barred.**

Bartender or **Barkeep,** a barman.

Baseball, great game in Canada and the United States; played with a ball and bat on an open field marked with a diamond ninety feet square, known as the infield. The indefinite extension of lines on adjacent sides of this square marks off the outfield from the foul ground. There are nine men in a team.

Basket social, a church or school event towards which individuals or families contribute baskets of eatables and delicacies. Picnics are conducted in the same way.

Basement, the underground or cellar flat of a building. Where a still lower flat exists, it is known as the **sub-basement.** (See **Sub-basement**).

Bat, hit, strike; as **bat you on the block,** hit you on the head.

Batch, to live the life of a bachelor. The lonely homesteader who has not yet taken unto himself a wife may say he is still **keeping batch,** or the man whose wife is absent from home may say he is **batching** it.

Batty, nutty, dippy, an eccentric person, one who acts the fool.

Bay State, Massachusetts.

Beach-comber, a settler on some island in the Pacific, usually a runaway seaman or a deserter from a whaler, and living a somewhat piratical life; or a sea-shore loafer, on the look-out for odd jobs.

Bead. To **draw a bead on him,** to attack with firearms, or even with a roasting speech.

Beano, or **Beanfeast,** a jollification or a feast.

Bears, operators on the Stock Exchange who are trying to lower prices.

Bear State, Arkansas, though California and Kentucky have also been sometimes given the nickname.

Beat, get along. **I'll beat,** I'll be off. **I'll beat off home,** I'll go home. When a hobo or tramp is en route to another town, by stolen railway rides or any other means, he is said to be beating his way. **Beat it,** get out, be off.

Beat the band. To indicate that strenuous effort is being made, a person will say "We're working to beat the band." "Matilda Muggins, pure as any dove, Awoke one night from sweet dreams of love, And saw within the moonlight near her bed, A spirit writing in a book of red. In words of flame it wrote, with mien inspired. 'What names are those?' the damsel then inquired. The spirit, answering, stayed its gleaming pen. 'The maids whose beauty fires the hearts of men.' 'And am I one?' she queried. 'Nay, not so,' The spirit said. Matilda spake more low, But hopeful still, and begged in accents bland, 'Write me as one that cooks to beat the band. The spirit wrote and vanished. The next night, It came again with a great scroll of white, And showed the names whose praise of men had blessed, And lo! Matilda's name led all the rest."

Beaver, an amphibious quadruped. with short ears, a blunt nose, small fore feet, large hind feet, and a flat ovate tail. Its fur is of great value.

Beaver, a man engaged on road-making near the lumber camps. **Buck beaver,** the foreman on such work.

Bed-rock, the solid rock underlying superficial and other formations. To **get down to bed-rock,** to get to the bottom of matters, to thoroughly understand.

Bee line, straight line of route to a given point. Naturalists say that when a bee is well laden, it makes a direct flight for home.

Beeves, cattle for slaughter. A word used in the Chicago stockyards and in the cattle market reports. One hears of **beef cattle,** which are animals being reared and fattened for the butchers or the jungle.

Behooves means the same as the Old-Country **behoves,** but is nearly always spelt with a double "o."

Bell-boy, the youth who would be called a page-boy in the Old-Country. He shows hotel guests to their rooms and thereafter is always on hand to answer the bell and supply the guests with what they ring for.

Bell-hop, slang for bell-boy. (See **Bell-boy**).

Bells. Getting there with bells on, getting there in time and in good form, or fit and hearty.

Belly-aching, grumbling, growling, in the throes of labour over some real or imaginary trouble. A person who goes **belly-aching around** is, as a rule, obsessed with some more or less imaginary cause of discontent, and in the process of getting the grouch off his mind absorbs considerable time, to the annoyance of all reasonably cheerful people.

Bender, a dissipation.

Best bet, something that looks good; while something that is uncommonly good is described as **the one best bet.** A young man may even be heard to speak of his sweetheart as his **one best bet.**

Bet, a word used in scores of phrases uttered by some Canadians in the course of conversation, in affirming or contradicting some statement. **You bet** (with emphasis on the pronoun), that's so, you're correct there, no doubt about that, you may be certain of that; or, **Bet you do, Bet you don't, Bet your life, Bet your boots, Bet your bottom dollar,** etc., etc. **On your life,** or **Not on your life,** is a variation of some of the above.

Big Bend State, Tennessee. The people coming from that State are sometimes called **Mudheads.**

Biggest toad in the puddle, the leader or chief, either in connection with politics or the rougher avocations of Western life.

Big noise, person or people boasting or rejoicing. "We are keeping quiet at present: the other fellows are **the big noise.**"

Big stick, the power of the law; a phrase originated by Theodore Roosevelt, who, referring to methods for dealing with the big trusts, said they should speak softly but use the big stick.

Biled shirt, or **Boiled shirt,** a starched white shirt, a full-dress shirt, supposed to be abhorred by dwellers in the Western camps.

Bilingual (adj.), in two languages, or possessing the command of two languages. In the educational system of Western Canada, **bilingual schools** are established for the benefit of foreign-born or foreign-speaking children.

Biscuit-shooter, a restaurant waitress.

Bit, the old 12½-cent piece of the United States was called a **bit,** and a defaced 20-cent piece was termed a **long bit,** while the old York shilling of Canada, valued at 12½ cents, was also known as a **bit.**

Bite, to snap at, to rise to the bait. "It was a palpable swindle, but everybody **bit,** and they were **severely stung.**" (See **Stung**).

Bitten, stung, taken in. (See **Stung**).

Blackfeet, a famous tribe of Indians.

Blaze. When a woodsman strikes out on a new trail into the virgin forest, he marks his pathway by chipping a few inches of bark from prominent trees on his right and left, thus indicating the way for others to follow or to guide himself back to the main trail. **Blazed trail,** a trail that has been so marked.

Blamed, a euphemism for blessed, blowed, or damned.

Blanket order, a wholesale order which, to make up the bulk required to bring it within the scope of special terms, permits the merchant some license to fill up with an assortment of other saleable goods very similar to the kind first specified.

Bleachers, the unsheltered seats at sports or on athletic grounds.

Blew in, or **Blew out,** a facetious way of speaking of a person's chance arrival or departure.

Blizzard, a snowstorm accompanied by a fierce wind; though, when the temperature has gone down to 20 or 30 below zero any mild windstorm bites hard enough to be called a blizzard.

Block, the house property lying between two streets. A person inquiring for a certain street will be told that it is so many blocks further on. Large apartment and office buildings are also called blocks, as, for instance, the MacIntyre Block in Winnipeg, or the Winch Block in Vancouver.

Block, head; as, **knock your block off,** knock your head off.

Bloods, a tribe of Indians.

Blow-hard, a boaster, a four-flusher. (See **Four-flusher**).

Blow-in, to spend or waste money. Money wasted or spent in drink or in a wasteful way is said to have been **blown.**

Blue Hen State, Delaware. The people from that State are nicknamed **Blue Hen's Chickens.**

Blue Law State, Connecticut; also **Land of Steady Habits,** the latter on account of the excellent morals of the people.

Blue nose, a native of Nova Scotia, after a potato of that name which Nova Scotians declare to be the best in the world.

Blue ruin, gin. (See **Drink**).

Blue sky securities, investments which are lovely to look upon from the wild-catter's point of view, but which may ultimately prove as unprofitable as acreage in the sky or castles in the air.

Bluff. In other lands, a **bluff** is a high, steep bank; but in Canada it means a cluster of trees on the prairie (for example, **poplar bluff**).

Bluff (verb), to overawe or alarm a person by pretence of special knowledge, strength or power. To **bluff,** in the game of poker, is to deceive, or gain an advantage by leading the other players to suppose that your hand is more valuable than it actually is.

Boarder, a person who has food, or boards, at a house. (See **Lodger** and **Roomer**).

Board measure, the amount of one-inch lumber in a plank, log, or square timber. Besides inch stuff, plank or scantling is usually sold by board measure, a foot of board measure being 1 foot long, 1 foot high and 1 inch thick.

Bobolink, the popular name of the ricebird or redbird, an American singing bird.

Bobsleigh, a sleigh on two sets of short runners, which **bob** over obstacles.

Bogus, anything pretending to be that which it is not, such as bogus titles.

Boiled shirt, or **Biled shirt,** a starched white shirt.

Bone, one of the names given to a dollar. Two bones, three bones, and so on. **Throwing the bones,** throwing the dice.

Bonehead, a thickhead, all bone and no brains.

Boneyard, one of the numerous facetious names given to the cemetery.

Bonspiel, a curling tournament.

Boob, soft guy, a simpleton, an easy victim for the artful ones. **Booby,** about the same meaning, viz., a weak-minded or idiotic person. **Booby asylum,** a madhouse.

Booby trap, any artifice by which mischief-loving boys enjoy themselves at the expense of their elders or other unpopular boys. They are common about Hallowe'en, and are thus frequently called **Hallowe'en tricks,** though they are of the kind that would be practised in the Old-Country on the morning of All Fools' Day.

Boodle, money, graft.

Boodler, a person who is after the boodle, or money; a grafter, or a person who works the political game for the profits and perquisites.

Boom, to advertise, to push, to puff, to boost. (See **Boost**).

Boom, heavy logs or timber chained together and thrown across a river to collect the drive of lumber, or to encircle the drive and hold it at anchorage. **Pocket boom,** a smaller collection of lumber which will ultimately be merged in the big boom preparatory to floating down-stream to the lumber mill.

Boom-stick, one of the long stretch of poles, chained together, which encircles a raft of logs while lying in a river or on the way down from the logging-camp to the lumber mill.

Boost, to laud, praise, advertise, boom; the opposite of **knock.** Canadians boost their country, their town, and everything they set their hands to, and the newcomer ultimately falls into the habit. "Do you know there's lots o' people settin' 'round in every town, Growling like a broody chicken, knockin' every good thing down? Don't you be that kind o' cattle, 'cause they ain't no use on earth, You just be a booster rooster, crow and boost for all you're worth. If your town needs boostin', boost her; don't hold back and wait and see If some other fellow's willin'—sail right in, this country's free. No one's got a mortgage on it, it's just yours as much as his, If your town is shy on boosters, you get in the boostin' biz. If things just don't seem to suit you, and the world seems kinder wrong, What's the matter with a-boostin', just to help the thing along. 'Cause if things should stop agoin', we'd be in a sorry plight; You just keep that horn a-blowin'—Boost er up with all your might. If you know some fellow's failin's, just forget 'em, 'cause, you know, That same fellow's got some good points— them's the ones you want to show. 'Cast your loaves out on the waters, they'll come back' 's a sayin' true; Maybe, too, they'll come back buttered, when some fellow boosts for you."

Boots, a word that is only applied to articles of footwear that come up over the calf of the leg. What are described as boots in the Old-Country are known as **high shoes** in Canada. (See **Shoes**).

Booze, a word which was good English in the fourteenth century, coming from the Dutch word "buyzen," to tipple; but which is now more vulgarly used in reference to any kind of intoxicating drink. To **booze** is to drink continually until drunk, or nearly so. **Booze-fighter,** an habitual drinker. **Hit the booze,** started a drinking bout.

Boss, foreman, manager, employer. Usually the chief man on a job, the person who does the employing and the fireing. (See **Fire**).

Bottom dollar, the last dollar. To **bet one's bottom dollar** is to risk all one possesses.

Boulevard. There are boulevards in Canada just as in France and England, but the word **boulevard** is chiefly and technically used in reference to the intervening strip of grass between the sidewalk and the roadway, the said **boulevard** being, of course, adorned with trees.

Bounced, discharged, sacked, fired; dismissed without ceremony.

Bouquet, a compliment, a tribute, a glowing testimonial.

Bowery, a district of New York, mention of which suggests vice and vulgarity.

Bowie-knife, a long sheath-knife or dagger used by hunters and others when the West was wilder than it is to-day. So named after Col. James Bowie, the inventor.

Boys, a general term to indicate one's companions, colleagues, or employees. "A bunch of the boys" is a common expression.

Brainstorm, an attack of madness, and the person so affected is sometimes called a **brainstorm.**

Brand. (See **Cattle brand**).

Brandy smash, an American drink, made of brandy and crushed ice.

Brass tacks, apparently the fundamental basis of all argument. An instance of the use of the words is found in a sermonette recently delivered by the "Man on the Street," a facile writer in the "Winnipeg Telegram." "Did you ever take notice how Christ placed emphasis on childhood and made use of youthful innocence to illustrate His teachings? He had mighty little use for money and money-lenders, for philosophers and savants, politicians and wiseacres. When He wanted to get down to **brass tacks** He cast wealth and ambition and glory and pomp and circumstance into the melting pot of the heart. Over and over again He declared that unless the grown man and woman humbled themselves to the innocence of the child they could not be counted as among the inheritors of His kingdom."

Brave, an Indian warrior, or an Indian of fighting age.

Break (verb), to plough or break up new land.

Breath. Change your breath, advice to change your tone or manner, and usually conveying a threat.

Bright and early, a phrase which the Canadian uses in announcing that he was on the job in good time. Perhaps he got out of bed earlier than usual that morning, and he **was up bright and early;** or he was at the meeting-place in good time, and he **was there bright and early;** or he was at the church before the bride, and he **was there bright and early. Bright and early** apparently means that he was there so early that there was time to spare.

British Columbia, the western Maritime Province of the Dominion, with an area variously set down from 375,000 to 395,000 square miles. Vancouver is its most important city and commercial metropolis, and Victoria, the city situated on the southeast of Vancouver Island, is the capital and seat of Government.

Brogans, a word of Irish origin, but in frequent use to describe the strong course shoes in use among field workers and labourers.

Broke, without money, penniless. **Stoney broke** is a variation or intensification of the description.

Broken, an adjective applied to land which has recently been reclaimed from its wild state and prepared for crops.

Brome, a succulent forage grass.

Broncho, a wild, half-broken horse; usually applied to horses that buck and show other signs of vice or make a fight against being mounted and ridden. **Broncho-buster,** a broncho-tamer or breaker-in.

Broncho, also an Englishman who still clings to Old-Country manners and speech; so called because he requires some "breaking-in." When he has been "broken-in," he may be described as an **Improved Britisher.**

Brush-pile, the refuse heap of the prairie farm, consisting of brushwood that is useless as fuel.

B.S. The initials of a very vulgar but common ejaculation, describing a story as lies and nonsense.

Buck, another name for a dollar.

Buck, a male Indian, a brave.

Buck beaver, the foreman over the men engaged in road-making near the lumber camps. (See **Beaver**).

Buckboard, a four-wheeled vehicle in which elastic boards, extending from axle to axle and upon which the seat rests, take the place of the ordinary springs. Seldom seen in Canada now.

Bucker, a bad, vicious brute of a horse; an animal that is "sure bad." (See **Broncho**).

Bucket shop, a stock gambling establishment. When lotteries were declared illegal in the States, places for the sale of lottery tickets were opened by negroes, and, as the police made unexpected raids, a bucket was kept ready at one notorious establishment to receive the tickets, and this, when turned upside down, was used as a seat for the apparently guileless proprietor, a long time transpiring before this simple trick was discovered. The name has gradually become wider in its meaning, and is now generally used for swindling stock brokers and their place of business.

Buckeye, an immigrant from Ohio, the **Buckeye State.**

Buckle of the Wheat Belt, a euphemistic name given to Winnipeg because of its preponderating trade, but other cities quite centrally situated on the great Canadian wheat belt also claim the title. (See **Wheat belt**).

Buckwheat, a grain in appearance between red fife and maize. Its flour excels in pancakes rather than in light bread.

Bud, a young girl "just out," who has left her schoolmates behind and has been formally introduced to the society circles in which her parents move.

Buffalo robe, an immense rug used when driving or sleighing. Formerly they were buffalo skins, tanned on one side and the hair left on the other; but the robes of the present day are generally made of cloth merely resembling buffalo skins.

Bugaboo, a bugbear, an idle fear or fancy that haunts and alarms a person.

Buggy, a light vehicle, generally with but one seat, and drawn by one or two horses. It has or has not a top, according to the weather.

Bughouse, apparently a noun, but generally used as an adjective, as "He is bughouse," he is mad, or crazy.

Bulge, advantage. "Medicine has always the bulge on the faith cure."

Bull-cook, a handy-man in a lumber camp, who carries water, splits wood, and does other chores, especially assisting the cookees.

Bull-dose, to bully, coerce; also sometimes means dosing a person with a false or extravagant view. The term is of Southern political origin, referring to a combination of negroes to insure the success of an election by violent or any means. **Bull-doser,** a bully or swaggerer.

Bull-headed, an adjective used in referring to a stupid person who says and does things in a thoughtless or reckless fashion; it may also be used to describe the actions of a brave man who takes unnecessary risks.

Bullion State, Missouri. The people are known as Pukes.

Bulls, operators on the Stock Exchange who are trying to boost prices.

Bull-whacker, a cowboy, a cowpuncher. (See **Cowboy**).

Bully, good, capital. **Had a bully time,** had a good time. **That's bully,** that's first-class. **Bully for you** is a commendatory exclamation.

Bummer, in the early days of California a person who sat or idled about the hotels or saloons; a loafer; one who sponged on his acquaint-

ances. The word is now contracted into **Bum,** and is in very common use in Canada where it means the impecunious man who loafs about hotels and saloons to put himself in the way of free drinks; but it is also used as an adjective to describe anything that is not truly genuine. An unreliable timekeeper is a **bum clock,** an unsatisfactory midday meal a **bum dinner,** a poor cigar a **bum smoke,** an inefficient workman a **bum workman,** a badly-stocked shop a **bum store,** and so on. When things are in that condition, they are said to be **"on the bum,"** and cadging is described as **bumming.**

Bun, a drinking fit, a jag, a tank.

Bunch, a group, a party. **A bunch of** the boys, a lot of the boys, or the word may be used in reference to any small crowd or party. A **bunch of horses** may easily be supposed to refer to a string of horses, and a **bunch of houses** may have reference to a row of houses or a small village. The reporter made his meaning perfectly clear when he stated that a certain railway accident had resulted in a **bunch of widows. Bunch** takes the place of the Old-Country word **batch.**

Bunch of niggers. Another exemplification of the use of the word **bunch** is found in the asseveration, "We're working like a bunch of niggers."

Bunco, to impose on, to fool, to hand out bunkum.

Bunco-steerer, a swindler, or confidence-trick man. "The bunco-steerer will find you out the morning after you land. He will accost you—very friendly, wonderfully friendly—when you come out of your hotel, by your name and he will remind you—which is most surprising, considering you never set eyes on his face before—how you have dined together in Cincinnati, or it may be Orleans, or perhaps San Francisco, because he finds out where you came from last; and he will shake hands with you; and he will propose a drink; and he will pay for that drink; and presently he will take you somewhere else, among his pals, and he will strip you so clean" (Besant and Rice).

Bunk, that part of a roughly-constructed sleigh on which the box or load rests.

Bunk, the box-like bed long known in the seamen's quarters on board ship, and later in the bunk-houses of the lumber camps.

Bunk-house, the men's sleeping quarters in a lumber camp.

Bunkum, false sentiments in speaking or writing. The use of the word is ascribed originally to a member of the United States Congress, Felix Walker, from Buncombe county, North Carolina, who, when his fellow members could not understand why he was making a speech, explained that he was merely talking for Buncombe:

Bunter, a foreman, or push; one who pushes the work along in a lumber camp or elsewhere.

Burg, a town or village. Probably derived from the Scotch word **burgh** or the English **borough.**

Bursar, a college secretary-treasurer. In Old-Country colleges and universities he is known as the **registrar.**

Bury the hatchet. (See **Hatchet**).

Bush, the forest or timber land, what once on a day was known as the backwoods. (See **Backwoods**).

Bushwhacker, a term occasionally used to denote a ne'er-do-well bush-worker; also used as a term of reproach for desperadoes in the Southern States.

Business college, a school of shorthand, type-writing, bookkeeping, and the several other things that help in a business career. **Business colleges** may now be found in all the large towns and cities.

Bust (verb), break up, smash, ruin. **Bust** also means, to be spent up, or broken financially. **On the bust** is "on the drink."

Busy. Get busy, make a start, get going, look lively.

Butt in, interfere, put your word in, put your oar in. To butt in usually means to interfere in a matter which does not claim your attention.

Butt-log, the largest portion of the tree, or that nearest the root and of greatest circumference.

By gum! an innocent-sounding variation of a profane exclamation.

C

Caboodle, an inclusive term meaning everything and everybody concerned. The enraged cowboy who threatened to **clean out the whole caboodle** probably had a mind to throw the saloon and its occupants into the street.

Caboose, a car, usually having a lookout, attached to a freight or construction train for the use of the conductor and rear brakemen.

Cache (verb), to hide, to stow away secretly; as, "a quart of rye was cached in the haystack." **Cache,** as a noun, means the place in which the article is hidden. A word derived from the French and much in use among gold miners.

Cahoots. To **go in cahoots** is to go in shares.

Calculate. (See **I guess**).

Calgary, the largest and most important city in the Province of Alberta, on the main through coast to coast line of the C.P.R., and the grand divisional railway centre between Winnipeg and Vancouver.

Californian widow, a married woman whose husband is absent, a grass widow. The expression originated at the time of the Californian gold fever, when many men went West, leaving their wives and families behind them.

Calk-shoes, shoes worn by lumberjacks, with spikes or calks in the soles, to prevent the wearer from slipping on the logs. Sometimes called **cork-shoes.**

Calumet (n.), the tobacco-pipe of the Indians, smoked as a symbol of peace, or to ratify a treaty.

Can, a drinking fit. **Canned,** drunk.

Can, to discharge a worker. **Canned,** discharged, fired.

Candy kid, a term of endearment for a child, presumably that likes candy; also used in reference to a girl or young woman, who also presumably likes candy or sweets.

Canned, discharged from employment, fired, sacked. **Canned** also describes a person who is drunk.

Canned music, player pianos, gramophones, musical boxes, etc.

Canoe, a light boat, narrow in the beam, and propelled by paddles. Once generally used by the Indians, but now much used by all as a pleasure boat on the rivers and lakes.

Canon, a term applied to the long and narrow mountain gorges or deep ravines in the Rocky Mountains.

Cant-hook, an iron-clad staff-like tool used in the lumber camps in the rolling of logs.

Canuck (or **Kanuck**), a Canadian.

Canvas-back, a kind of duck, greatly valued for the delicacy of its flesh.

Canyon, same as **Canon,** which see.

Capacity, holding power, amount of room. In a case where the Old-Country reporter would describe the hall or meeting-place as "filled to its utmost capacity," the Canadian scribe would merely say "it was filled to capacity."

Cape Diamond, the point in the St. Lawrence on which Quebec stands.

Caption, the title or heading of a newspaper or magazine article.

Caribou, reindeer that are well known in Canada and that also frequent the barren lands of the Arctic regions.

Carpenter, a man who is fully qualified to do first-class work in that trade. **Rough carpenter,** one who has less knowledge of the trade, but is entrusted with rough work at a low scale of pay.

Cash in, to die, or to "hand in your checks."

Casquet, a coffin. **Casquet factory,** works in which casquets or coffins are manufactured. The word is in general use.

Catch colt, a foal of unknown paternity.

Catch crop, a crop which, under favourable climatic conditions, is obtained from land intended for fallow, from seed fallen on ground of previous year's crop.

Catnip, a plant, or herb, like mint; and supposed to be old folks' favorite tea.

Cat's light, the dusk or twilight; or, in the language of the Scottish poet, "between the gloamin' and the mirk."

Cattle brand, the mark of ownership placed on farm or on range cattle with a red-hot iron, and ranchers protect their live-stock property by registering their brand-mark at the Provincial Department of Agriculture. Strayed animals are thus more easily returned to their proper owners.

Cattleman, a rancher; though the word applies in a general way to anyone engaged in the rearing or selling of cattle for slaughter.

Cayuse, a broncho or Indian pony, originally bred by the Cayuse Indians.

Cent, Canadian coin about the size and value of a British halfpenny.

Centennial State, Colorado; the people being sometimes also called **Centennials.**

Chairwoman, as applied to a woman who presides at a meeting, is being dropped. The force of usage has made **chairman** quite admissible with reference to a woman.

Challenge has the same meaning as in the Old-Country, but is most frequently used in reference to challenging, or objecting to, a juror or a voter. The **challenging** process is a long and tedious proceeding in such cases.

Chambermaid in a livery barn, an hostler.

Chapel, composed of Union men employed in a printing office, the **chapel** being the court at which purely office questions of wages and conditions are first discussed, and chapel meetings are usually held after the jig. (See **Jig**).

Chaps (pronounced **shaps**), leather leggings or breeches (without a seat) worn by cowboys to protect their legs from becoming chafed from friction in the saddle. One can imagine how tweed or cloth pants work up to the knees from constant bobbing up and down, and the folds in pants thus formed will soon skin a rider's legs. Proper **chaps** are not skins or thin leather, but thick leather that will not crease. Many cowboys appear to favor **bearskin chaps.**

Chaser, a non-intoxicating drink taken to **chase down** the more fiery spirits. The confirmed soak usually, however, **chases** one drink down without another of the same stuff.

Cheap, paltry, inferior.

Cheap guy, a mean person, always looking for as much as possible for as little as possible.

Cheapjohn, a paltry person. Oftener, however, used as an adjective signifying petty or paltry; as, **cheapjohn politicians.**

Check, a bank cheque. Many firms of high standing, however, still use the English spelling of the word.

Checks. Hand in your checks, to die, to "cash in."

Chestnut, an old or stale joke.

Chestnut bell, a tiny toy which even old-timers scarcely remember, but which had a great vogue in its day. The "boys" hung them beneath the lapels of their coats and set them tinkling the moment they discovered they were having a chestnut handed out to them.

Chew. Let us chew, an invitation to dine or have a meal.

Chewing-gum, in appearance like a lozenge, with a thin shell of sweets, inside of which is the stuff to keep the jaws in motion. It consists of a natural gum resin, as spruce-gum, or an artificial preparation of chicle, paraffine, etc.

Chilcotens, a tribe of Indians; habitat, British Columbia.

Chin (verb), to chatter, or work the chin in idle conversation. A drygoods salesman was requested by his employer to do less **chinning** and more selling.

Chink, a Chinaman.

Chinook, an Indian tribe located in the State of Washington; also a dialect composed of a jargon of Indian, English, French, etc., which was used in intercourse between the various tribes and the white traders in the North-West.

Chinook winds, warm and pleasant winds which sometimes prevail on the eastern slopes of the Rocky Mountains, which carry the warmth of the Japanese current from the Pacific Ocean through the mountain passes and eastward out on the plains, thus modifying the winter climate of Alberta.

Chipmunk, a small, striped squirrel.

Chokecherry, a small red cherry which turns dark blue or black when ripe. Eaten when ripe, it leaves a parched choking feeling in the mouth. Its juice makes a popular wine. They are frequently called **chokeberries** in error; but it should be remembered that the **chokecherry** contains a stone, and that **berries** contain seeds.

Chores (natural ch sound), daily duties in the home, odd jobs about the house.

Chore boy, the errand boy, or the boy who does "any old job" about a house or office.

Christy stiff, a hard felt hat.

Chuck, food, grub, victuals; though, as in the Old-Country, most frequently applied to bread.

Chute, an inclined trough-like construction down which articles or people may slide. **Chutes** of various designs are an adjunct of all large Canadian schools as a fire-escape, and young Canucks are particularly partial to fire practice.

Cinch (pronounced **sinch**), an easy task, a soft job, something easily accomplished, winning or earning money easily **That's a cinch,** that's a certainty, or that's easy. **Cinch**

(11)

(verb), to earn, win, capture, make certain of. The **cinch** in a horse's trappings is the saddle-girth.

Cincinnati olive, a pig. **Cincinnati oyster**, a pig's trotter.

Citizen. (See **Naturalisation**).

City, population qualification, 10,000.

Claim, the patch of land staked out by the prospector or the gold-miner in accordance with mining laws.

Clam, certain bivalvular shellfish which are used as food, and notably as a stew known as **Clam chowder.**

Clawhammer coat, a swallow-tailed coat, with tapering skirt or tails.

Clean up the town. (See **Shoot up the town**).

Clerk, a store assistant, salesman or counter-man. The man who attends to the books in the counting-room is a bookkeeper or accountant.

Clock, a semi-contemptuous way of speaking of a watch, especially an Old-Country article wound up with a key, stem-winders being the prevailing fashion in Canada.

Club, the policeman's weapon of defence on occasions when the threatened danger does not call for the use of the revolver. **Clubbing** the crowd, on occasion, has afforded much enjoyment to police in certain American and Canadian cities.

C.N.R., Canadian Northern Railway.

Coal is found in Alberta and in British Columbia. According to one authority, British Columbia's coal measures are sufficient to supply the world for centuries; and, according to another authority, "there can never be a fuel famine in Alberta as long as there are miners left to dig coal out of the earth and cars to haul it to the consumers."

Coal oil, the lighting oil known in the Old-Country as paraffin oil.

Coasting. (See **Tobogganning**).

Cobalting, wild-catting, or promoting hazardous money-making schemes, the district of Cobalt having once been notorious for over-exploitation. (See **Wild-cat**).

Cocklebur, a coarse weed with a prickly fruit.

Cocktail, a mysterious concoction of the drinking saloons, the component parts varying in different parts of the Western Hemisphere.

C.O.D., cash on delivery.

Codland, Newfoundland.

Coffin nails, cigarettes.

Coldest day that has been registered at the Government Observatory in Winnipeg was 53.5 below zero, on December 24, 1875.

Cold feet, a person who suffers from cold feet is one who is easily discouraged, faint-hearted, or afraid to push forward an enterprise. A person who is lethargic or devoid of pushfulness is said to suffer from cold feet; as is also the man who moons around instead of going

ahead. The expression is used among the sporting fraternity in reference to a man who gets ahead of the game and wants to get away before he loses his "velvet."

Cold-snap, the most common way of referring to a long or short spell of severe frost. "When the frigid Arctic breezes Touch your spine, despite your clothes; When old Winter's artists paint you Blue, and leave a crimson nose; Why, you should not get excited, Though chilblains arouse your ire, But just amble to the basement And help nurse the furnace fire. There is consolation for you, Though the water pipe has burst, And you've frozen ears and fingers, And you think this **snap's** the worst, For down in sunny Africa, Where there's never snow or sleet, A million folks are suffering With the itchy, prickly heat."

Collins. (See **John Collins**).

Colonist car, the car in which immigrants make their railway journey to the West, holding the place of third-class carriages on Old-Country lines. (See **Pullman** and **Tourist**).

Come-back, a champion who had relinquished sport, but comes back to the game and makes good. When he fails to succeed, he is a **gone-back.**

Come off, an exclamation one hears when he has made some extraordinary statement or when his story is exciting the envy of his listeners. Ah, come off is apparently an instruction to come down from the speech platform or off the liars' stool.

Come-on, a derisive term applied by the knockers to any promising speculation; but especially in the case of a subdivision where building lots have been sold to first-comers on particularly easy terms so that they may invite others to come on. (See **Knockers** and **Subdivision**).

Comfort station, a public lavatory.

Conductor, the official in charge of a passenger train.

Cone, a word well-known to the young folks of Canada, especially when preceded by the words "ice-cream," an **ice-cream cone** usually being uppermost in their minds when a nickel is in sight. The **cone** itself is composed of crisp biscuit work and is consumed with the ice-cream.

Confederation. The Provinces constituting the Dominion of Canada entered into Confederation at various times: Ontario, Quebec, New Brunswick and Nova Scotia, on July 1, 1867; Manitoba, July 15, 1870; British Columbia, July 20, 1871; New Brunswick, July 1, 1873; Saskatchewan and Alberta, September 1, 1905.

Con man, the individual who plays the confidence trick. **Con talk**, the confiding stories told by the con man.

Conservative, as an adjective, always qualifies the word **estimate,** the speaker or writer apparently meaning that it is a most accurate and careful estimate. Politically, Conservatives are Imperialists and the party which stands for Canada as an integral portion of the British Empire.

Continental, a mild swear-word. "I don't care a **continental**" is the way it is usually uttered.

Cookee, a cook or assistant cook in a lumber camp or with a railway construction gang.

Cookstove, a portable fireplace specially constructed for cooking purposes, of which there are many varieties, from the tiny article that "boils the kettle" to the magnificent piece of ironmongery that will cook anything from the baby's midnight lunch to the evening dinner of the Gourmands' Club.

Coon, abbreviation of **Racoon** (which see); also a common name for a negro.

Coop, the police station; or, to be more exact, the cells in the police station.

Cord, a measure of cubic contents, 128 cubic feet, equivalent to a pile 4x4x8 feet. **Cordwood,** wood intended for fuel, and sold by the cord as above.

Corduroys, poles placed on swampy ground in the work of making a logging road from the lumber camp to the river or the railway.

Cork-boots. (See **Calk-shoes.**)

Corker, one not easily beaten. A **Corking good man,** better than the best. A **Corking speech,** beyond contradiction, or a capital speech.

Corncracker State, Kentucky. **Corncrackers,** immigrants from Kentucky.

Corntossle, a farmer or other countryman, unused to city life.

Corral, a fenced place where ranch cattle or horses are gathered in. **Corralled,** rounded up, gathered in.

Cost of living. The following were retail prices at Winnipeg in March, 1913: Bacon 25c. per lb., beef 14c., bread 5c., butter up to 45c., cheese 20c., coal per ton (2,000 lbs.) $11.00, coal oil 30c., coffee 40c., eggs (per dozen) 35c., fish, fresh, 15c.-18c., flour 4c., lard 20c., milk (per quart) 10c., mutton, 22c.-25c., pork (salt) 20c., potatoes (per bushel) 75c., rice 5c., sugar 6 2/3c., starch 10c., tea 40c., vinegar 15c., wood (per cord) $8.50, rent varies greatly. The rent of a house in Winnipeg of 4 to 6 rooms may be anywhere from $15.00 to $50.00 per month.

Cough up, pay up, stump up, disgorge; a slangy way of demanding restitution or payment of a debt.

Coulee, a ravine or deep gully. The names of some Canadian towns include the word, such as Plum Coulee, in Manitoba.

Cowboy, the picturesque individual, famed in song and story, who does the herding and other work on a horse or cattle ranch, often called a **cow-puncher,** though the latter name is also given to the men who work on the cattle boats plying between North America and the Old-Country.

Cowcatcher, a framework contrivance placed in front of a locomotive for removing obstructions on the railway, such as strayed cattle.

Cow grease, butter.

Cow juice, milk. At table, the request to **Pass the cow** means that the cream or the milk jug is wanted.

Cowman, a rancher or a cowboy. The word is, however, only used jokingly or when offence is intended.

Coyote, the prairie wolf, a dejected-looking animal a little less than a small collie. They still abound, and are seen even within a few miles of such a city as Winnipeg.

C.P.R., Canadian Pacific Railway.

Crab-apple, a wild, sour fruit.

Crackerjack, a rare good fellow who excels in every work and accomplishment, and wins the admiration of everyone; also anything that is first-class, as, for instance, a crackerjack programme or a crackerjack game.

Cracker State, Georgia. The people are spoken of as **Crackers.**

Crap, or **Craps,** a game with dice, notoriously a gambler's infatuation.

Crazy, the word most commonly used in describing an eccentric person. If you complain about the quality or cooking of your food, the Canadian Hebe will possibly tell you that **you** are crazy.

Creek, a small river, an inlet, a recess or small bay in the shore of the sea or of a river.

Crees, a noted Indian tribe.

Creole State, Louisiana.

Crib, a raft of square timber or ties, laid layer upon layer, each layer crossing the one beneath, and girt by a chain or stout rope.

Cubby-hole, the space under staircases or beneath the sloping roof of an attic, sometimes used as a box closet or cupboard, and having a fascination for children in their games of hide-and-seek.

Currency, properly the coin or paper money of the Dominion, though United States silver coins are also in frequent use in Canada, and for the time being are regarded as currency.

Cuspidor, a spittoon, which in Canadian hotels is quite an ornamental utensil.

Custom tailor, a high-class tailor or clothier, dealing with the best class of customers, and supplying only made-to-measure garments.

Cut, cut down, fell. A **season's cut** in a lumber camp is a season's output; and standing trees marked out for future operations may be spoken of as next season's cut.

Cut it out, be done with it, give it up, cease it. A reformed man, referring to his late evil habits will say, "I have cut them out;" a person referring to an undesirable acquaintance says, "I've cut him out; I've got no more use for him;" a merchant referring to an abandoned department of his business will say, "I have cut it out." The words are used in connection with almost anything that has been abandoned or given up. Again, they are heard as a protest against banter or unruly conduct, when the person suffering annoyance will exclaim, **"Oh, cut it out!"**

Cute, neat, natty, something novel and smart.

Cuts no ice, a common metaphor meaning that some speech or effort has no effect or leaves no impression. **Cuts no grass** has a similar meaning.

Cutter. (See **Sleigh**).

Cutting up dog, acting foolishly.

D

Dad, frequently used when addressing an elderly man, as "Hello, Dad!"

Dago, an Italian.

Dam, an obstruction on a river, placed there to hold the water back, and so fill the upper reaches or to hold the timber from the adjacent clearings until the time comes for the big drive down stream to the lumber mills.

Dandy, tip top, swell, up to the mark. If a Canadian has anything to sell it is quite certain, in his estimation, to be a dandy.

Dangle, a word used in some of the lumber camps, and meaning to **get,** or **get out.** The boss's order to a man he is firing may be **You can dangle.**

Date, an assignment, an engagement. The Western damsel who seeks an excuse when being "asked out," or who wishes to impress a suppliant with the fact that she is much "sought after," will say she has already **a date on** for that special day or evening.

Deadhead, a person who occupies a theatre seat on free admission or who travels by train or boat on a free pass.

Deadheads, in the lumber trade, are logs which have been sunk in the rivers or lakes. After long years of this seasoning, they become valuable for many purposes, and fully repay the cost of the dredging for them.

Dead men, a term for whiskey or beer bottles after they are emptied of their contents.

Deck, a pack of cards.

Deck. On deck, on the spot, ready for duty or for action.

Delinquency, the word used in juvenile court proceedings when referring to a child's offence, with the humane object of avoiding the word "crime."

Den, a bachelor's apartment, or some cosy little room where lodgers assemble to worship My Lady Nicotine and swop stories. A girl of spirit may also call her own little apartment her **den.**

Deport, to banish from Canada. An undesirable immigrant may be sent back to his country of origin, at the expense of the shipping company which carried him westward, any time up till he has been three years in the Dominion. Drunkenness and loss of intellect are the chief reasons for deportation.

Depot, a railway station.

Derby, a bowler, or hard felt hat.

Devil-dodger, a sky pilot, a parson.

Dewlap, the loose skin that hangs from the neck of an ox, a cow, or other animal similarly constructed.

D.G.S., Dominion Government Survey, the work of marking off townships, sections, half-sections, and quarter-sections of Dominion land.

Diamond State, Delaware.

Dicker, to bargain, barter, quibble, play with. Generally applied to a deal in small articles.

Different, frequently means **novel or unique.** An athlete who performed some feats **distinctly different** gave a show unlike anything seen before, and a storekeeper who advertised his goods as **different,** meant that he had variety and quality found nowhere else.

Digger, a saddle horse.

Dinky, small, neat, natty, cute.

Dime, a ten-cent piece.

Dippy, weak in the head, nutty, silly.

Discipline, besides being used as a noun, is also used as a verb, meaning: to censure, to reprimand, to punish, for a blunder or neglect of duty. "Ship's officer disciplined" was the heading over a newspaper paragraph which announced that a captain's certificate had been suspended for neglect of duty.

Discriminate, to make a distinction between, to select from others. An employee who is not having a square deal, or who is discharged for some reason best known to his employer, may allege that he is being **discriminated against.**

Distances. Quebec to Liverpool (by Belle Isle route) 2625 miles, Quebec to Liverpool (by Cape Race route) 2875 miles, Quebec to Glasgow (by Cape Race route) 2563 miles, Quebec to Winnipeg 1596 miles.

Ditched, in the ditch; the usual position of a locomotive or railway train after it has run off the line. In the Prairie Provinces at least, derailed trains have seldom a chance to run into an embankment.

Dive, an immoral house. To describe such a place, the word is more frequently used than it is in England.

Divide, the height of land marking the boundary of river basins. **The Great Divide,** eternity.

Doc, abbreviation of "doctor," very generally used in addressing a doctor of medicine, a veterinary surgeon, or a dentist.

Doctor. (See **You're the doctor**).

Dodgers, small handbills intended for distribution on the streets, where the passers-bye may attempt to **dodge** the distributor; or for "fly-posting" in the manner of the Old-Country, when the "fly-poster" may have to **dodge** the owner of the property or the hoarding where he sticks up his **dodgers.**

Does things, an expressive phrase that is used in reference to a man of action. The man of whom it is said that **he does things** gets up the ladder in quick time and frequently helps a few others up with him. The man who **does things** is in great demand **when things have to be done right.**

Dog-gone, a form of mild swearing, with little or no meaning.

Dog's nose, a mixture of beer and gin.

Dog train, the picturesque cavalcade which accompanies Arctic travellers and traders, viz., a number of sleds, each drawn by a string of dogs.

Dollar, variously known **as a simo**leon, a one-spot, a toadskin, a greenback, a plunk, a bone, a buck, a bean, etc. A five-dollar bill is sometimes called a V.

Dollar mark, $. Authorities are not agreed as to the origin of the dollar mark, though probably it is an elaboration of the figure 8, and denoting a piece of eight parts or bits, into which the dollar was formerly divided. (See **Bit**).

Dominion Day, July 1, a Dominion holiday commemorating the confederation of the provinces.

Dope, any drug surreptitiously dropped into a man's drink, usually preliminary to being robbed. The word is also applied to reading matter or a tale of tiresome and foolish nature. To **dope** a person is to drug him, and a man who lives in a state of chronic alcoholism is termed a **dope.**

Dope fiend, a drunkard, or a man addicted to the use of drink, dope or drugs.

Dough, a vulgar name for money or wealth.

Doughnut, a small round cake, made of flour, eggs, and sugar, and boiled in lard.

Dough-slinger, cook in a lumber or railway construction camp; also known as **cookee, stomach-robber,** etc.

Doukhobors, a religious body of immigrants who have put Socialism into everyday practice, paying all earnings into the common fund and sharing everything in common.

Down and out, utterly defeated or completely beggared; cast down and knocked out of the game or out of former associations.

Down East, an indefinite expression used by Westerners in referring to some place in the East, though it usually means somewhere in Ontario.

Down the line. When a man pays a visit to the immoral quarter of the town, he is said to have been **down the line.**

Downtown, the business section of a town or city.

Down to the ground, an American expression; as, "That suits me **down to the ground.**"

Doxology works, a church, chapel or mission hall.

Draw a bead. (See **Bead**).

Drink. Among the numerous **names** given to intoxicants of the various kinds are—appetizer, aqua vitae, ball of fire, belly vengeance, blue ruin, bosom friend, bottled earthquake, breakey-leg, bucket, bumper, bung juice, cheerer, cinder, digester, dope, drain, eye-opener, facer, fiz, flip, forty-rod lightning, gargle, grapple the rails, hard stuff, heeltap, hell broth, invigorator, John Barleycorn, kill-the-beggar, liquid fire, lotion, nightcap, nip, old man's milk, pill, poison, refresher, rot-gut, rouser, settler, shout, slight sensation, smile, something, soother, soothing syrup, soul destroyer, sparkler, stimulant, stingo, strip-me-naked, swig, taste, tanglefoot, tipple, toothful, etc. **Invitations to imbibe** may be held out in any one of the following forms— Let us stimulate! What'll you take? Nominate your pizen! Will you irrigate! Let's drive another nail! What's your medicine? Let's liquor up! Will you try a smile? Let's see a man about a dog! Try a little Indian! etc. **Responses** to an invitation are likely to be made in words somewhat as follows—Here's how! Here's at you! Don't care if I do! I'm that! Yes, siree! Anything to oblige! I'm with you! Count me in! Count me as one of the boys!

Drink hearty a convivial invitation when the cup is at the lip.

Drive, the conveying of logs or timber down the river to the lumber mills. A **drive** generally consists of the collected result of a season's cut by one firm and perhaps from several camps on the same stream.

Drop. To have the drop on a person is to have him at the point of your revolver, probably with **hands up,** or his hands placed flat on the table across which the argument is proceeding. The party of the first part (who has the drop) is thus in a position to dictate terms or drop some lead into the system of the party of the second part should be attempt to reach for his gun. In more peaceful circles, to **have the drop** on a person is to have some advantage over him, or to have him somewhat in your power.

Drop letter, a letter intended for delivery from the posting office, or in the same city or town in which it was posted. A 1-cent stamp then suffices for the usual 2-cent letter.

Drover, a general name for the person who goes about the country buying fat cattle and hogs.

Drummer, a commercial traveller or outside salesman.

Drunk. The village drunk, or town drunk, is the title jocularly given to some individual who has qualified, or is apparently qualifying, for that distinction.

Dry, the condition of a town in which Prohibition law is in force, where no alcoholic drinks are permitted to enter. (See **Wet**).

Dry farming, husbanding rather than dissipating the fertility of the soil; or, applying practical methods, such as summer fallowing, to overcome a deficient precipitation.

Dry goods, merchandise, men's and women's apparel, bed and table linen, cloth, blankets, curtains, carpets, etc.

D.T., a popular abbreviation of **delirium tremens.**

Dub, a slow, stupid specimen of humanity.

Dude, a fop. There are not many in the West, but occasionally one blows in from London or New York.

Dudelette, a mentally and physically stunted male, of any age, to whom dress—and frequently overdressing—is the Alpha and Omega of life. Almost invariably it is used in conjunction with the word **Semi-ready** (thus, **Semi-ready dudelette**), because one generally finds such dressy individuals do not, as a rule, patronise the best custom tailors; but, rather, purchase garments of ephemeral style and of the semi-ready type. (See **Semi-ready**).

Duds, clothes, clothing; one of the many words imported from Scotland, and now heard even more frequently in Canada than in the land of its nativity.

Dug-out, a hole in the ground, covered with rude framework and sod, used as a temporary dwelling, for storage, or (in some countries) as a cyclone-cellar. While the homesteader is erecting his shack a dug-out is very probably his place of habitation.

Dump, the scrap-heap, a supposititious last resting-place for old locomotives, men who are down and out, etc., etc.

Dust, gold, money; a word originating in the gold-mining camps, where gold dust was practically the currency.

Dust Blanket. The last act, or work, or treatment, in summer fallowing is to pulverize into dust the surface soil to the depth of one or two inches, which covering, or dust blanket, retains the moisture underneath it about the roots of the next growing crop.

Dutch. To Go Dutch is to let each man in a party pay for his own drink or refreshment.

Dutch treat, a form of conviviality considered remarkable because each man in the company pays for his own refreshment. (See **Go Dutch**).

E

Eagle, a United States gold coin of the value of ten dollars.

Ear-flap, that portion of a cap which may be turned downwards to protect the ears against frost.

Eat, to breakfast, dine, or sup, or, to have a meal. When about to have a meal, a Canadian will say "I'm going to eat"; or, in referring to the house at which he boards, he will say "I eat there." Again, meals are sometimes referred to as **eats,** and occasionally one may see a cafe with the signboard "Good eats here."

Eaton's, a familiar household word throughout Canada, and indicating the mammoth departmental stores at Toronto and Winnipeg founded by Timothy Eaton.

Edmonton, capital of the Province of Alberta, and the trade-distributing centre of a district which stretches northward to the Arctic circle. Many new-comers make the mistake of supposing that Calgary, the more central and more advertised city, is the capital of the Province, but Edmonton holds on to the honour of seat of Government.

Effete East, a hackneyed phrase meaning "the worn-out, exhausted Eastern Provinces." But the Westerner who jokingly refers to the East in this fashion seldom means it: he has a warm corner in his heart for some well-remembered spot 'way back in Ontario or in the Maritime Provinces.

Eleemosynary, a fine-sounding word that has a great future before it. Some pedantic Western company promoter once introduced it into a company's articles of incorporation, and it has had a great vogue ever since. It means **charitable.**

Elevator. (See **Grain elevator**).

Eliminate, one of the pet words of the Canadian reporter and public speaker, and used in the most extraordinary places, usually, however, meaning "leave out," "cut out," or "drop."

Empire State, New York. The people are known as **Knickerbockers.**

Ence or ense. Words with these terminations, such as **defence** and **expense,** are correctly spelled just as they are in the Old-Country, though, through carelessness, the wrong spellings have got into the newspapers until they have become almost the custom.

End of steel, just that point in a new country to which railway construction has advanced. **End of steel** (with name of railway or new branch) thus appears in the list of post offices, and assumes the importance of a village or town.

Engine hostler, an employee in a railroad roundhouse, who overhauls the locomotives between trips and prepares them for going out on the road.

E pluribus unum, the motto of the United States, meaning **One of many,** or **Many in one.**

Eskimo, or **Esquimau,** (pl. **Eskimos,** or **Esquimaux),** the tribes inhabiting the extreme northern shores and islands of Canada. **Eskimo dog,** a wolf-like animal, a native of the northern regions of Canada and Siberia, much used for drawing sleighs or sledges. The Eskimo sledge-dog is also called a **Husky.**

Esquimau. (See **Eskimo).**

Et al., contraction for the Latin words **et alii,** frequently seen in law reports and legal documents.

European plan. These words may be seen posted up in certain hotels, notifying that guests are charged as per the menu. That is, they pay for bedroom according to the accommodation and just those meals they order or eat. (See **American plan).**

Express, parcel delivery service. The carriage of parcels is conducted by **express** companies having close business relationship with the railway companies.

Extensive farming, grazing and grain-growing on a large scale. (See **Intensive).**

Eye-Opener, a characteristically Western journal published at Calgary and circulating all over Canada. Edited by R. C. Edwards, it is chiefly famous for the audacious fashion in which it scores friends and foes alike, and for its screamingly funny contributions to Western wit and humour.

F

Fall, autumn, the fall of the year.

Fall and **Fell** find a place in several characteristic Canadian phrases bearing reference to duping, deceiving or being imposed on; as, for instance, "the philanthropist **fell for** the starving family story," "the cute city editor **fell for** a piece of false news and inserted it in his paper," or "the defaulting clerk gave a very plausible excuse for his default, and his employer **fell for** it." The person thus deceived or imposed on is the **fall guy.**

Fallow, a word used to describe land left idle for a year on account of its lack of fertility or on account of noxious weeds. Such land receives extra preparation for the next year's crop.

Fandango, lively proceedings of a joyous nature, though a saloon riot may also be referred to as a fandango. Originally, a **fandango** meant a lively Spanish dance with much musical accompaniment.

Fans, sports promoters or enthusiasts; critical and expert followers of the game.

Fan-tan, a gambling game notorious among the Chinese. It is played with cards or dominoes.

Feed, a word used also as a noun and meaning food, as in the case of **horse feed, cattle feed,** etc. A **seed and feed merchant** is one who sells seed for gardens and fields and food for horses and cattle.

Feet. (See **Cold feet).**

Feet. Got there with both feet, got there in a hurry, bent on business, or in a determined frame of mind. **Put both feet down,** made his determination clear, would stand for no humbug.

Fellow, a term of address applied to a man, not necessarily offensively, but usually implying that he who uses it does not care whether it offends or not; as, "Say, fellow." When used in the plural it is less liable to be interpreted offensively; as, "Say, fellows, let's hit the trail."

Fest, a suffix for many words, as **Talkfest,** a conference, or a feast of words; **Gamefest,** a sports tournament; **Songfest,** a feast of song, etc., etc.

Fiend, a word frequently used in conjunction with other words; as, **dope fiend,** a drunkard, or a man addicted to the use of drink, dope or drugs; or, **crap fiend,** a person addicted to the dice game, etc.

Fierce, describes anything from a person's objectionable conduct to a violent storm. **"It's fierce"** is applied to any unsatisfactory state of affairs. Women, perhaps, use the word more frequently than men; and may find it handy to describe a rival's new hat or her personal appearance. "Val," said a homely old dame to her young protegee, "I want to tell you right now that you was sure the queen of the ball; everybody said you looked jest like a queen in a picture, and I never heard a word against your low-neck dress. It looked all right on you, don't you see? On me, for instance, it would a been **something fierce."**

Fill the bill, supply all that is wanted or expected. **Can fill the bill** are the words with which a Canadian will assure a client, a customer, a prospective employer or others, that he can do the job right and on time.

Fire-break. (See **Fireguard).**

Fire-fighters, the picturesque title given to the men who battled with the great prairie fires and now quite commonly used by the Western reporter in reference to the fire

brigade men or others who contend with the flames either in the city or on the prairie.

Fire-bug, an incendiary, a mischievous person who wilfully sets fire to property.

Fire chief, official title of the chief officer of a fire brigade or of the fire-fighters.

Fired, discharged from a situation; equivalent to the Old-Country expression, "got the sack."

Fire-fly, a winged luminous insect that is in evidence after dark. Pat and Mike, fresh from the Emerald Isle, tired after a day's travel on foot, sought refuge from the mosquitoes under a hay-stack. In the darkness Pat espied a fire-fly, and declared to Mike that the mosquitoes were after him again, with lanterns.

Fireguard, as known on the Western range and farm lands, is usually an embankment of earth thrown up, fence-like, round farm buildings or crops, to stop the advance of a prairie fire. A fireguard is also formed by ploughing up a strip of land on each side of the property requiring protection.

Fire-hall, a fire station, the headquarters or branch establishment of the fire brigade. (See **Fire-fighters**).

Fire-ranger, a person whose duty it is to prevent outbreaks of forest or prairie fires.

Fire water, the name which Indians formerly gave to whiskey and other intoxicating drink.

Flag-station, a spot at which there is no railway agent regularly on duty, but at which trains drop or take up passengers on signal of a flag.

Flapjacks, the pancakes of the western camps and the Eve-less homesteads. They are, of course, of generous size, but "it's very seldom there are any left."

Flat rate, the same price all round.

Flim-flam, an idle, worthless story; hot air.

Float, a large dray, or rolley; but the word is generally used in reference to a dray used in a procession to exhibit working models or people engaged in some industry.

F.O.B., free on board. Exporters on F. O. B. terms are liable for all charges on board steamer at port of shipment. Consignees pay sea freight and other charges on arrival of goods.

Foothills. The natural features of Alberta combine the beauties of prairie and mountain scenery. For three hundred miles open and wooded plains stretch out in vast level reaches, and then climb over softly rounded mounds that grow higher and sharper till they break into jagged points and serried ridges and at last rest upon the base of the Rocky Mountains. These rounded hills that join the mountains to the prairies are called the foothills. They are so distinctive and unique a feature of the country that Alberta is known as the Foothills Province.

Footings, the immense stones, laid next to mother earth, upon which the foundation walls of buildings are reared.

Fool, foolish. Freely used as an adjective, as **fool** play, **fool** exhibition, **fool** conduct, etc.

Foot the bill, to pay up; though the expression is generally used in reference to paying another person's debt. A person may also say he can foot the bill when he undertakes to do another person a service or take up a situation satisfactorily.

Footwear. (See **Rubbers, Overshoes, Moccasins**). Snow-shoes (which see) are not articles of footwear, but used in the pastime of snowshoeing.

Foreclose, to take possession of mortgaged property when the borrower has failed in his payments.

Forest-ranger, a forest guardian, or a person whose duty it is to prevent the stealing of timber.

Fork of the trails, the spot at which one trail breaks into two, one trail trending to the right and the other to the left. Geometricians might give it a more mystifying name, but lovers of the romantic West will still call it the **fork of the trails.**

Fort Garry, a trading post and settlers' depot on the western bank of the Red River, at its junction with the Assiniboine, built after the union of the rival fur companies in 1821. A stronger fort, with stone walls, bastions, and port-holes, was put up in 1853. All that remains of this historic structure is a gateway, now one of the sights of Winnipeg.

Forty-rod, or **Forty-rod lightning,** whiskey so fiery that it is calculated to kill at forty rods distance, or on sight.

Four-eyed, spectacled. The cowboy said he "never had no use for **four-eyed** school-ma'ams; but exceptions have to be made in every rule; and the new girl down to the school is certainly a peach."

Four-flusher, a boaster, a blow-hard. (See **Blow-hard.**)

Frame house, or **dwelling,** one built entirely of wood, or lumber, but usually, of course, with a brick or stone foundation.

Frame-up, usually a dodge in the political game, though the expression is used in reference to any plot or shady scheme. **Framed up,** worked up. The words are also used in reference to a person's manner of tackling a job, when it may be said "He **framed up** well," or badly, as the case may be.

Franchise, a right or privilege, a charter; as, a street-railway franchise.

Freeze up. What is known as the **Freeze up** is that period of the year when frost, snow and ice have put an end to nearly all outdoor work and closed up the rivers for navigation. Since 1888 the earliest freeze up of the Red River at Winnipeg was November 3, in 1910, and the latest opening on April 23, in 1904. The latest freeze up of the Red River was December 3, 1899, and the earliest opening March 20, 1910.

Freight, goods in transit. **Freight train,** a goods train; also **freight boat, freight wagon,** etc.

Freight. The word is also used in reference to the carrying charges. Whereas in the Old-Country the question would be "What's to pay?" in Canada it is "What's the freight?"

Fresh, nasty, saucy, arrogant, quarrelsome. "Don't get fresh with the boys: you only make them stubborn."

Freshet, the unusual flow of water on a river after a thaw or heavy rain.

Frieslander, immigrants who hail from Friesland, the most northerly province of Holland.

Frisco, the short name for San Francisco.

Frontier, a word frequently used in romances of the American West and meaning the frontier of civilization, or the point to which Cousin Jonathan's troops had advanced and had frequent encounters with the Indians.

Frost-bite. New-comers' first experience of this is likely to be on the ears, nose, the cheeks, or the chin. The immediate common remedy is rubbing the affected spot with snow, and thereafter consulting a wise old-timer. Prompt action is necessary, but on no account apply hot water or go up against the stove.

Funds. (See **In funds**).

Funerals. During the winter months, when the ground is frozen, the first portion of the ceremony is the placing of the coffined remains in the cemetery morgue. The final interment takes place in the spring, when the ground has softened sufficiently to permit the digging of graves.

Fyle, Fyled, a reversion to the old form of the words **file** and **filed,** used in reference to the safeguarding of letters or documents.

G

Gabfest, a feast of talk, or a gathering of people possessed of the "gift o' the gab."

Gait, speed or pace at which an individual or an animal is going. A storekeeper advertises that his store is going at **a great gait,** meaning that he is doing great business.

Galician (pronounced **Galeechian**), actually an immigrant from the north-eastern part of Austria; but generally immigrants from any part of Central Europe are dubbed as **Galicians.** Excavators and navvies are usually **Galicians.**

Gall, nerve, cheek.

Galoot, an awkward, uncouth youth. The word is used in both a friendly and unfriendly sense.

Gang-saw, a saw with four to twelve blades working together as a jig-saw, thus able to cut up a log in one forward movement, slicing the log into 1 inch or 2 inch board; called "gang" saw because working together.

Gangster, a member of a gang or crowd of roughs. Party organs find the word useful in describing there opponents.

Garbage, kitchen or household refuse.

Garbage can, the receptacle in which city-dwellers deposit their kitchen and household refuse for removal to the nuisance ground or the incinerator.

Garden State, Kansas; also sometimes spoken of as the **Squatter State.**

Garnishee, a legal process by which wages or money owing to a debtor must not be entirely paid over to him until he has satisfied his creditors.

Gauntlets. (See **Mitts**).

Gay, quarrelsome, overbearing, displaying temper. The word **fresh** is used in the same sense. "Lord, help me at my humble job today. Th' foreman thinks I'm nothin' but a dog; An' with that tongue he's always gettin' gay—Say, I could lay him flatter than a log."

Gazook, a familiarity, the nearest approach to which is found in the exclamation, "Oh, you goose!"

Gee, a common exclamation somewhat equivalent to the English "By Jove." **Gee whiz,** a variation of the above.

Geese known to Canadians are of several varieties. The Wavey or Snow Goose and the Honker or Canadian Goose are the best-known species. There is also the Hutchings Goose or small Canadian Goose, marked just like the Honker, and the small Grey Goose or Laughing Goose. All these, with the exception of the Honker, are Arctic birds.

Geewhilikens, an exclamation of surprise.

General Delivery, the Poste Restante, or department in a post office where immigrants or visitors may call for their letters. Thus, if John Smith were emigrating to Winnipeg, and had no address in that city, he should instruct his friends to address him "John Smith, General Delivery, Winnipeg, Manitoba."

Get-away, an escape; as "His get-away was complete; and the police are without a clue as to his whereabouts."

Get-rich-quick, a combination of words used in an adjectival sense and usually referring to dishonest schemes for making money.

Getting wise. (See **Wise**).

Gets there, attains his object. **Gets there every time** refers to a person who succeeds in all his undertakings. "The June bug has a gaudy wing; The lightning bug a flame; The bed bug has no wings at all, But he gets there just the same."

Get-up-and-get, or **Git-up-and-git,** an expression used as a noun and meaning purposefulness or energy; as, "The son has all the **get-up-and-get** that the father was endowed with."

Gilt-edged, first-class, best of its kind. **Gilt-edge securities,** safe and profitable stocks, shares, or investments.

Gimme, pronounced either in one syllable or in two, and meaning **give me. Lemme** (let me) is a word constructed on the same principle of contraction.

Ginger up, wake up, stir yourself, get moving, look lively.

Gink, which, being interpreted, means, a **fool,** an **idiot,** or an **ass.**

Glad hand, a welcome, a friendly reception. Winnipeg aspires to become a great convention city, and offers the glad hand to all mankind.

Glad rags, or **Joy rags,** a person's best suit or Sunday clothes.

Go. (See **It's a go**).

Goat, the scapegoat. A number of people may be all equally responsible for some blunder or mischief, but the blame is fastened to one individual only, and that person is described as **the goat. The goat** may even be wholly innocent.

Goat. To **get his goat** is to ruffle a person's temper. **You can't get my goat** is the declaration of a person who resolutely refuses to be disturbed by badgering or chaffing. "Mary had a little lamb, Which often was contrary; It followed her to school one day—'That **gets my goat'** said Mary."

Gob-stick, a silver spoon or fork.

Go-cart, a child's mail-cart. The young Canadian also gives the name of **go-cart** to the old box he mounts on wheels and does chores with, or runs errands. In winter, strips of steel (runners) take the place of the wheels and the go-cart becomes a **sled.** (See **Sled**).

God's Own Country, a name frequently given to the Dominion by patriotic Canadians and satisfied settlers.

Go Dutch. To **Go Dutch** is for each person in the company to pay for his own treat or refreshment. See **Dutch Treat**).

Gold brick, a very promising speculation or investment which afterwards turns out to be a fraud or failure.

Gold-bug, a man of wealth, a millionaire.

Golden State, California.

Gold mine, any profitable investment, from a fish and chips shop to a speculation involving millions.

Good is used in a variety of ways. To **Make good** is to do well or come up to expectations in one's employment; **I feel good,** I feel well; **Looks good,** it looks all right; **Sounds good,** sounds all right (sometimes a doubtful compliment); and **Good and strong, good and early, good and plenty,** etc. When the mercury is away up in the nineties, it is **good and hot;** and when it is in the twenties or thirties down below, it is **good and cold;** and, most amusing to the newcomer, the man who is very ill is **good and bad.** The laugh, however, is against the newcomer if he criticises such phraseology too severely, for, in the Old-Country has he not been accustomed to speak of a sick person as **pretty bad,** or of an ill-favoured face as **pretty ugly?**

Goods, the article wanted. A Canadian or American who would imply that he has what you want, the cash to pay for an article, the qualifications for a situation, or anything and everything in request, will say "I've got the goods," or "I can deliver the goods."

Good standing, full standing. Members of a society, union, or other organization, who have paid up all dues or indebtedness, who are clear on the books, and who have complied with all the conditions of membership, are described as members **in good standing.**

Good time, an enjoyable experience. A man who has been having a riotous time, and has possibly lost or "blewed" his wad, is also derisively told that he has had a good time.

Gopher, the name given to several breeds of burrowing animals which infest the North-West. These little quadrupeds, which honeycomb the earth, have large cheek pouches extending from the mouth to the shoulders, incisors protruding beyond the lips, and broad, mole-like forefeet.

Gopher State, Minnesota.

Gospel factory, an irreverent term for a church or chapel.

Go the whole pile, to put all one's bank on a solitary and despairing chance; a phrase which had its origin in the piles of gold dust used as circulating medium by gambling miners in the Western gold days.

Gotten, a reversion to the old form of the word got; as, **has gotten hold of it, has gotten there in time.**

Grade (n.), a road, and presumably a new road just constructed across newly-broken ground.

Grade (verb), to cut out and level a roadway; also to adjudge the quality of grain, classifying it into its different grades.

Grade. Make the grade, make the running. A foreman may ask a workman, "Did you make the grade?" meaning thereby, "Did you complete the work satisfactorily and on time?"

Grader, a person who grades or prepares the new roadways; a powerful mechanical device, like a plough, to assist in grading or road-making.

Graft, bribery and corruption; money or benefits extorted or received by a person drest in a little brief authority. **Grafter,** a person who uses his position to fill his purse or who sells posts and employment to the highest bidder. "Graft means exactly what you choose to make it. A salary for sinecure is graft. A wide-open expense account is graft. Anything or everything that pertains to money or perquisites not accounted for by the stern value-received rule is graft."

Grain elevator, the high, towering erection for the storage of grain seen near most of the railway stations in the wheat-growing provinces. The largest elevator in the world is that of the Canadian Northern Railway Company at Port Arthur, Ontario, with a capacity of 7,500,000 bushels.

Graingrower, a person growing grain exclusively, and usually extensively.

Granite State, New Hampshire.

Grass widow, a married woman whose husband is absent. **Grass widower** is also used in reference to the husband when the wife is absent on duty or on a holiday.

Greased lightning, terrific speed.

Greaser, a Mexican, or other Spanish-American; sometimes called a **Coffee-cooler,** his favorite beverage being cold coffee.

Great White Way (The), the uptown section of New York famed for costly hotels and glittering amusements.

Greenback, a dollar. The paper money issued in the United States during the Civil War was known as **greenbacks.** The term was originally applied only to the bills for small amounts, which were backed with green, but ultimately, in both Canada and the States, the one word represented bills of all values.

Greenie, a tenderfoot, a new arrival in a Western camp.

Green Mountain State, Vermont.

Gridiron, the United States flag, the Stars and Stripes; also **Gridiron and Doughboys.** The **Goose and Gridiron** refers to the Eagle in conjunction with the flag. The words are, however, more in use on board ship than on land.

Grip, a travelling bag or suit-case, and presumably that portion of one's luggage that is carried by hand and kept in close grip when crooks are about.

Grit, strength and perseverance. Politically a Grit is a Liberal.

Grouch, a persistent grumbler, one who is never satisfied. **Has a grouch on,** is in a bad temper. **Grouchy,** fault-finding.

Ground floor. To get in on the ground floor is to join in a speculation on equal terms with the promoters of the scheme.

Grouser, a gurmbler, a grouch, a person who complains about anything and everything. An army word imported from the Old-Country and Canadianised.

Grub, food, provisions; an Old-Country word that is in quite common use.

Grubstake, a word commonly used and meaning sufficient money ahead to prospect or size-up the situation. Thus many firms or bosses give a grubstake to their men.

G.T.P., Grand Trunk Pacific Railway.

Guest. All visitors or residents in an hotel are **guests,** and **register** by signing their names in the **guest-book** in the **office,** a department usually fixed opposite the main entrance.

Guff, windy talk designed to deceive; an incredible stiry.

Gulch, a narrow passage in the mountains, a pathway between rocks.

Gulf State, Florida.

Gully, a narrow passage in the mountains, a ravine or hollow worn by water.

Gum tree. Up a gum tree, in an awkward fix, or "all up with him."

Gun, a general name for pistols, revolvers and rifles. The larger weapon is usually referred to as a shot-gun. **Gun men,** those who actually do, or are supposed to, carry revolvers.

Gunning, shooting. **Going out gunning,** going out on a shooting expedition.

Gut-wagon, the sleigh on which the mid-day meal is conveyed from the camp to the lumberjacks working in distant parts of the woods.

Guy. A wise guy, one who poses as the possessor of superior wisdom, and usually reckoned as a fool.

H

Hack, a cab. But hacks are going out of fashion as rapidly in Canada as they are in the Old-Country.

Hail, as it is sometimes known in Canada, is a force to be reckoned with. Hailstorms are occasionally so destructive that the insurance companies charge a special rate for havoc caused thereby.

Half-breed, half-blooded, usually the progeny of a white father and an Indian or Esquimau mother.

Half-sprung, the words most commonly used to describe a man who is showing signs of liquor. **Half-shot** is similarly used.

Hallowe'en, the eve of All-Hallows, and observed in many Canadian homes just as it is in the Old-Country; but more frequently it is made the occasion for all kinds of pranks, innocent or malicious, against individuals and property, rendering it something akin to a Guy Fawkes celebration or an All Fools' Day demonstration.

Ham-tree orchard, an illusory trade proposition or speculation. Legend hath it that some smart real-estater once sent a bunch of speculators hunting for an orchard where hams grew upon the trees.

Hand it. This is how the words are sometimes used: "That story will do to tell women and children, but don't hand it to me, old scout." Or the man who protests that he does not squeal when bad luck comes his way may say, "I take what's **handed out** to me." **Hand,** in most utterances, simply means **give** or **gave,** and that which is **handed,** or **handed out,** may be anything, tangible or intangible.

Handle, to deal in. A wholesaler or retailer, in speaking of the articles he trades in, will say he **handles** these things.

Hang-out, a person's place of residence, the club or other place he frequents most frequently, or (perhaps the most correct meaning) the place where he is most likely to be found when wanted.

Happened along, happened to come that way.

Happy hunting ground, the future abode; from the Indian's idea of heaven.

Happy right. "You're happy right" means entire approval of what has been said. An expression that is becoming obsolete.

Has-been, a person of the down-and-out class, one who boasts of a glorious past but is no good now. Such a person may sometimes be described as a **Never-was.**

Hash-slinger, a restaurant waiter or waitress.

Hatchet. To **bury the hatchet,** to cease strife, or to let bye-gones be bye-gones. To **dig up the hatchet,** to recall the cause of strife or to renew the quarrel. In the war-like days of the Indian tribes, certain symbolic ceremonies were connected with the war-hatchet or tomahawk, the burying of the weapon being symbolical of a declaration of peace, and the digging up being a symbol that hostilities were again to commence.

Hawk-eye State, Iowa; and the people are known as Hawk-eyes.

Hayseed, a derisive term which the city man will apply to a farm worker or other countryman unused to city life.

Haze, to play practical jokes upon a person. **Hazing** is one of the pastimes of college life in the Western Hemisphere, and the person **hazed** has often a very unpleasant experience. Cowboys may occasionally be heard using the word, to **haze** an animal apparently being to drive it in a direction out of its regular way.

H. B. C., Hudson's Bay Company, and also irreverently said to mean **Here Before Christ.**

Heart to heart talk, straight speaking. "Had a **heart to heart talk** with him," gave him a bit of my mind.

Heeler, a political worker, one who is at the heel of a political boss.

Heel-taps, leavings, liquor in the bottom of a glass.

Hefty, goodly, weighty, bulky; as, a hefty wad of dollar bills.

Hen fruit, eggs.

Highball, whiskey or brandy diluted with soda-water, ginger ale or some other effervescing liquid.

Highbinder, a political conspirator or blackmailer.

Highbrow, an intellectual person, or a person who affects intellectuality. A person of aesthetic tastes and manners is also nicknamed a highbrow.

Hike, to leave one place for another, on foot, as opposed to driving. In city life **"I'll hike,"** may mean "Im off," "I'm going," followed, perhaps, by the parting words, "So long."

Hired man, the handy-man about the house or farm. **Hired boy,** a young farm hand.

Hitching pole, a post to which a traveller may hitch his horse. They may not be seen in the great thoroughfares, of the West, where there is an abundance of telegraph and electric lighting poles; but in the streets of the quiet towns of Eastern Canada they have been planted firmly and frequently down both sides—usually within a few steps of a saloon door.

Hit the booze, taken to drinking. (See Booze).

Hit the breeze, to move on, to hit the trail, to hit the pike.

Hit the pike, to move on. (See Pike).

Hit the trail, to start on a journey by road. **Let's hit the trail,** "let us be moving," "let us get off to work," or "let us get back to camp."

Hive, to pack or change the boundaries of an electoral district to suit the purpose of the political party in power.

H.M.C.S., His Majesty's Canadian Ship. The letters may be seen on the cap-bands of seamen on the Canadian warships.

Hob. Playing hob with anything, such as a business, is simply playing ducks and drakes with it, as an Englishman would say; ruining it.

Hobbles, straps which fasten horses' front feet together to prevent them from travelling far over the prairie when on pasture. Hence the hobble skirt, which for a brief period was a craze among fashionable ladies.

Hobo, a tramp, a vagrant, a man of the type of Weary Willie and Tired Tim.

Hock, pawn, pawnshop.

Hockey, a game played with a club curved at the lower end, by two sides, each side striving to drive a block or disc, called the puck, into that part of the playing-field marked off as their opponents' goal. The Canadian winter game is played on a sheet of ice, and the players travel on skates. (See **Land**).

Hog (verb), to grab, or take all. "You mustn't **hog** it over me" was the younger son's warning when the first-born attempted to seize more than his share of the patrimony.

Hold down, keep, retain. To **hold down a job** is to be able to hold or keep it, being able to fulfil the duties.

Holding, land leased or bought, or timber rights acquired by lumbermen.

Hold-up, robbing by violence. A dishonest storekeeper or a swindling acquaintance is also described as a hold-up.

Holidays. The public statutory holidays in Canada are—Sundays, New Year's Day, the Epiphany, Good Friday, the Ascension, All Saints' Day, Conception Day, Easter Monday, Ash Wednesday, Christmas Day, the birthday (or day fixed by proclamation for celebration of birthday) of reigning Sovereign, Victoria Day, Dominion Day, Labor Day (the first Monday of September), and any day appointed by proclamation for a general fast or thanksgiving.

Holy smoke! an exclamation of surprise.

Home-seekers, a general term applied to immigrants and new arrivals in search of a new home or land whereon to settle.

Homesteader, a man who takes up and settles on a free grant of land. Any person who is the sole head of a family, or any male over 18 years old, may homestead a quarter-section of available Dominion land in Manitoba, Saskatchewan or Alberta. The applicant must appear in person at the Dominion Lands Agency or Sub-Agency for the District. Entry by proxy may be made at the office of any Local Agent of Dominion Lands (not sub-agent), on certain conditions, by father, mother, son, daughter, brother or sister of intending homesteader. Duties—Six months' residence upon and cultivation of the land in each of three years. A homesteader may live within nine miles of his homestead on a farm of at least eighty acres solely owned and occupied by him or by his father, mother, son, daughter, brother or sister. In certain districts a homesteader in good standing may pre-empt a quarter-section alongside his homestead. Price—$3 per acre. Duties—Must reside six months in each of six years from date of homestead entry (including time required to earn homestead patent) and cultivate 50 acres extra. A homesteader who has exhausted his homestead right and cannot obtain a pre-emption may take a purchased homestead in certain districts. Price $3 per acre. Duties—must reside six months in each of three years, cultivate 50 acres and erect a house worth $300. (See **Land**).

Homicide, the killing of one man by another. **Homicidal,** murderous.

Honest Injun! pledge of sincerity. Equivalent to "on my honour."

Honest to God! a declaration of truthfulness or sincerity, as in the opening line of Robert W. Service's Ballad of Pious Pete, "I tried to refine that neighbour of mine; honest to God, I did."

Honker, a certain species of goose, so called from its peculiar cry. (See **Goose**).

Hoodlum, a rowdy, a rough, a bully; and generally supposed to be men who operate in the shade of night.

Hoodoo, something that brings bad luck; the opposite of **mascot.**

Hooker, a glass of spirits.

Hoosier, an immigrant coming from the State of Indiana, or a native of that State.

Hopper, a grain reservoir. The huge grain elevators at Fort William are facetiously called the **hopper,** and the railways and lake boats, the **spout.** A heavy crop often causes congestion of the hopper and spout.

Horn, a drink of spirits. A Canadian sport will say "Come and have a horn."

Hornswoggle, to hoodwink, swindle, humbug, bamboozle. One sometimes hears the exclamation, "May I be eternally **hornswoggled!**"

Hostler. (See **Engine hostler**).

Hot air, windy talk, a speech with nothing in it, statements which are not believed, promises which will not be fulfilled. **Hot air artist,** one who excels in the hot air stunt. (See **Stunt**).

Hottest day ever registered in Winnipeg was 100.5, on June 23, 1900.

Housekeeping. Where rooms are advertised for **light housekeeping,** facilities are provided for preparing meagre meals, but laundry and heavy work is expected to be sent out.

House of Commons, the Lower Chamber of the Dominion Parliament. The Senate is the Upper Chamber.

How are they coming? Another of the peculiar ways of asking how you are doing or how you are getting along.

How's chances? what are the prospects? With this form of speech a Canadian may inquire for employment or anything else that he desires.

Hoyle. (See **According to Hoyle**).

Hub, or Hubby, a husband.

Hudson Bay route, a proposed new route to reduce the length of the journey between the wheat fields of the West and the markets of Europe. From various opinions, optimistic and the reverse, it is concluded that the route is open for navigation from about the 15th July to about 15th Oct. The C.N.R. have built a line from Winnipeg to The Pas on the Saskatchewan River. From there the Dominion Government will build a line to Fort Churchill, 465 miles, or Port Nelson, 397 miles. This route will effect an estimated savings of 970 miles on the distance from the Western wheat fields to the Atlantic seaboard.

Hudson's Bay Company, pioneer fur traders of Canada with great territorial possessions and now becoming famous as proprietors of large departmental stores.

Hudsonian, relating to Henry Hudson, the discoverer, or the bay which bears his name, or the Hudson Bay Company.

Hum, though much used in the Old-Country is a word of American origin, and means "to make things lively." To make a business hum is to stir it up and keep it bounding on successfully.

Hummer, a business, a performance, or anything else, that is "going strong."

Hump, move, get along. **Hump yourself,** get out, or get on your journey.

Hunch, a premonition, a presentiment, or an instinctive feeling for which one can give no reason. **Riding a hunch,** obeying the dictates of a hunch, or making yourself merry or miserable over the hunch.

Hung out his shingle, hung out his sign. Before the advent of the sign-writer or the brass-plate engraver, the hustling Westerner would chalk his name and trade on a shingle (or slate) and hang it outside his store or his primitive little office. Having hung out his shingle, he was ready for business.

Hurrah, a jubilation, celebration, a meeting or social to celebrate some event, such as a victory in sport.

Husky. (See Eskimo dog).

Hustle, to work hard, to make things look lively, especially in business. **Hustler,** the man who 'does things,' the man who spreads the infection to those around him, the man who gets on in Canada and elsewhere. "Hustle! and fortune awaits you; Shirk! and defeat is sure; For there's no chance Of deliverance For the chap who can't endure."

Hyphenated American, an Irish-American, a German-American, or other naturalized citizen of the States.

I

Ice, frozen water.

Iceberg, a large mass of ice detached from some Arctic or Antarctic glacier and which floats in the sea.

Ice-boat, a strong steamboat which gets busy near the opening of the navigation season, to clear a channel through the ice on the rivers.

Ice-cream, cream that has been flavored and frozen.

Ice-field, an extensive sheet of floating ice.

Ice-floe, a smaller field of floating ice.

Ice-house, a place for storing ice.

Ice-pack, a field of ice so closely packed that navigation is difficult or impossible.

Icicle, a pendent, conical mass of ice, formed by the freezing of dripping water, much in evidence around the eaves of Canadian houses when frost suceeds a thaw.

Igloo, the snow house of an Eskimo; also the excavation which a seal makes in the snow over its breathing hole, for the protection of its young.

I guess, I reckon, I calculate, are expressions imported from the States. and in frequent use in Canada. **Calculate** is common in the Western States, as "I calculate you are a stranger here;" New Englanders use the word **guess;** and **reckon** is of Virginian origin.

Improved Britisher, a person born in the Old-Country, but of long residence in Canada. Generally so described as a naive compliment to the Dominion.

Improved farm, cultivated or partly cultivated, and having some of the necessary buildings or barns on it. (See Wild farm).

In bad, not in favour, on bad terms. When the bartenders' union asked for the use of a certain meeting-place, "a request from such a source was naturally a command, for who would want to be **in bad** with the genial wine-clerk?"

Indemnity. Members of the Dominion and Provincial Parliaments are paid for their services, but, instead of the word "pay" or "salary," the word **indemnity** is used.

Indian, one of the aborigines of North America, so named by Columbus and others because they believed that the new lands discovered by them were part of the Indies. **Indian reserve,** a piece of territory specially reserved as a settlement for Indians and their families. There are many such reserves scattered throughout Canada.

Indian affairs engage the attention of a special department of the Canadian Government, with headquarters and a large staff at Ottawa, and with many agents, inspectors and other officials scattered throughout the provinces.

Indian list, the black list, or the list of interdicts, people who have been barred by the magistrates, on the request of an employer or near relative from purchasing drink or being supplied with drink. All Indians are supposed to be on the **list,** and any person supplying them with intoxicants is liable to a heavy fine.

Indian moccasins, the original Indian shoes or footwear, which are generally made of moose-hide, fit close, are soft and pliable, and are sometimes ornamented with beads. They are not on sale, for wear, at the large departmental stores; but may be bought at the Indian curiosity shops, and sometimes at stores in country parts near-bye an Indian reserve. (See **Moccasins**).

Indian summer, the period of mild weather which usually occurs between the first fall of snow and the regular outbreak of winter, during which period the Indian makes his final arrangements for the winter.

In funds, all right financially, or has cash in hand. **"I'm in funds"** is the utterance of the impecunious individual when he has rather more than his accustomed amount of cash: his normal condition is **stoney broke.**

Inning, an innings at cricket or other games. The final "s" is not used in Canada and the States.

Inside lots, a term used in the real estate business to indicate lots or property inside the city limits, or on land which must necessarily come within the city limits with the city's early expansion. (See **Outside lots**).

Intensive farming, mixed farming, raising a variety of small crops of a large number of things—everything possible on a farm, grain, grazing, dairying, vegtables. (See **Extensive farming**).

In the neck. (See **Neck**).

Irrigation, engineering devices for watering farm lands in seasons of drought. The semi-arid belt of Southern Alberta has special need for irrigation, and several wealthy companies have undertaken the work.

I should smile, I should say so. Sometimes it is varied in the words **I should say.** (Another importation from the States).

It's a go, it's a deal, it's a bargain, it's agreed on. **It's a go** may also mean that some scheme is working out satisfactorily. The committeeman, when asked how the arrangements for the dance were proceeding, replied: "It's a go; it's going to be some dance all right." (See **Some**).

I. T. U., International Typographical Union, which has some 60,000 members in Canada, the United States, Porto Rico, and the Philippine Islands.

It was to laugh, then we had to laugh, or, then it was time to laugh; a remark made on telling a joke or relating some ludicrous incident.

Ivories, a person's teeth, either real or false.

J

Jack-rabbit, a hare. A rabbit is usually given its correct name, but a hare is more frequently spoken of as a **jack-rabbit.**

Jag. Has a jag on, has a tank, is drinking heavily.

Jam, a block, or squeeze. In the lumber trade, during the **drive** of logs down stream, a jam sometimes occurs at a bend or in a narrow channel, and heroic effort is required to displace the **key-logs** and get the drive once more under way down stream.

Jamboree, one of the more euphemistic names for a drunk or a spree.

Jeans, overalls; though in light conversation a man may refer to his ordinary trousers as his jeans, and when he says that he has a "stack of gold in his jeans" he means that he has a pocketfull of cash or a very substantial wad of dollar bills.

Jig, in printing and certain other trades, means a day's work, or that period between starting and leaving off. A **Lobster-jig** is the spell of duty overlapping the day jig and the night jig, commencing in the afternoon and finishing about midnight.

Job. Putting a job over on him, playing a trick or a swindle on a person.

Jobber, a man who takes a contract for cutting timber or logs. Customarily, a jobber is paid a certain proportion of the agreed price as each stage of the work is completed—so much when the timber is cut; so much when it is **skidded** or piled; so much when it is stacked at the river, or banked; so much when the **drive** down the river is finished.

John Chinaman, a Chinaman, a Chink.

John Collins, a morning reviver composed of soda water, gin, sugar, lemon and ice.

Joint, an opium den, a gambling house, or a low-class saloon; though a house, cafe, or similar place may be called a joint, and it may be a **good joint** or a **bad joint.**

Jollied, chaffed out of some possession or betrayed into some admission. Another form of the confidence trick.

Jolly, to cajole, to wheedle, or (in the slang language of the Old-Country), to canoodle; to humour a person with the intention of ultimately deceiving him.

Jolt, a drink of spirits.

Josh, might be interpreted in the slang of the Old-Country as "kid" or "gammon."

Joy rags, one's best suit or go-to-meeting garments. Also called **glad rags.**

Joy ride, a pleasure drive, very often a reckless one.

Juice, the electric current. **Turn on the juice,** turn on the light, or turn on the power.

Jump is used in many expressions uttered in Canada. To **jump a job** is to leave without notice, and usually when work is proceeding; **jump the line** (or boundary) stealing across the international border line (or boundary) between Canada and the States, evading the customs and immigration regulations, etc. **Bounty jumper,** in the United States, was a man who, during the Civil War, would receive the bounty, join his regiment, and then decamp, to reappear in another State, to go through the same performance, in some cases many times over.

Jumpers. (See **Overalls**).

Jumping contract, non-fulfilment of an agreement.

Jump the track, to run off the line; referring, of course, to a railway train, though a person who has wandered from the paths of virtue, or has got beyond restraint, may also be said to have **jumped the track.**

Junk, second-hand goods, truck, rubbish. **Junk-shop,** a second-hand goods store.

K

Kale, money, or wealth.

Kanuck (or **Canuck**), a Canadian.

Keeps. Young Canuks play marbles for keeps, and the grown-ups sometimes decide the disputed possession of an article by tossing for keeps.

Keewatin (pronounced **Kee-way-tin**), a District of the North-west Territories, part of which lying south of the 60th parallel was, in 1912, divided and added to the Provinces of Manitoba and Ontario. Maps printed previous to 1912 show prosperous Manitoba like a mere "postage stamps," as it was nicknamed, stuck on the middle of the North American continent, but this extension of her territory gave her a great seaboard on Hudson Bay.

Kentucky colonel, a bogus colonel. After the American Civil War, it is alleged, nearly every man in Kentucky was either a captain, a colonel or a general.

Kerosene, a lamp oil, having the same uses as paraffin oil in the Old-Country, and highly explosive. "Stubborn fire, Weather keen; Cook Maria, Kerosene. Splendid fire, Brilliant light; Cook Maria, Angel bright."

Key-log. When a jam occurs during the drive of timber down stream to the lumber mills, it probably happens that one particular log, which has got out of the course or athwart the stream, is responsible for the hold-up. This is the **key-log,** and to get it directed on to the straight course, and the drive once again moving, is one of the most hazardous duties of the river lumberjack. (See **Jam**).

Keystone State, Pennsylvania, from the circumstance that when the names of the original thirteen States were arranged archwise in their geographical order, Pennsylvania occupied the position in the centre.

Kibosh. To put the **kibosh** on is to wind up, to stop, to silence, or to put the extinguisher on a person.

Kick, to complain, protest, grumble. **Kicker,** a persistent grumbler, or one who frequently **kicks** in defence of his rights. "There's a **kick** from Muggins & O'Reilly" means that the gentlemen mentioned have sent in a letter of complaint, and the person who is responsible for Messrs. Muggins & O'Reilly's dissatisfaction may reply that they 'don't have any **kick**," which means that they have no real grievance. "Smile and the world smiles with you; **Knock** and you go it alone; For the cheerful grin Will let you in Where the **kicker** is never known. **Kick,** and there's trouble brewing; Whistle, and life is gay, And the world's in tune Like a day in June, And the clouds all melt away."

Kickshaw, a choice morsel, a dainty savoury dish, a snack that tempts the appetite.

Kid, a child.

Killed his man, a phrase that may be regarded as somewhat synonymous with **Won his spurs.** In the old lawless days in Western America, the person of whom it was said that he **had killed his man** was respected among the **gun men** and the **bad men.** He had proved that he could use his weapon, and was seldom molested.

King's (or **Queen's**) **English,** the English language correctly written or spoken.

Knickerbockers, people from the State of New York, the Empire State.

Klooch, an Indian woman, a squaw.

Knock, to disparage, to discourage, to cry down. The opposite of **boost.** "Boost, and we are with you; knock, and you'll be alone."

Knocked up, in the Old-Country, means tired, jaded, done up, or laid aside with illness, but in Canada the words have a meaning which precludes their use in the presence of females.

Knocker, objector; a person habitually disposed to oppose or depreciate new movements, proposals or schemes; one who decries another person's work or efforts.

L

Lacrosse, a game which originated among the Indians and is now popular among Canadians. It is played with a ball and a crosse, or bat, somewhat similar in appearance to a tennis racquet. The object of the game is to drive or carry the ball with the crosse between and past two goalposts at the opposite ends of the field of play.

Lady of the Snows, a name bestowed upon Canada by Rudyard Kipling. **God's Own Country** is what the patriotic Canadian more frequently calls it.

Lagoon, a shallow lake near the sea or a river, formed by the overflowing or infiltration of the waters of the latter.

Lake State, Michigan. The people from Michigan are known as **Wolverines.**

Lam, hit, strike, lay out. "Every time I go to school, The teacher lams me with a rule. Makes no dif'rence if I am a fool; She's got to quit lamin' me with a rule!"

Land, in the Dominion of Canada, is laid off in square **townships,** each containing thirty-six sections of as nearly one square mile as the convergence of meridians permits. A section is divided into four quarter-sections, containing 160 acres each.

Land guide, a man appointed to guide homestead seekers to a suitable location.

Land-hunger, an obsession, often amounting to a disease, which sometimes attacks the successful settler. "Land, and still more land" is the chief aim and object of the life of a person so afflicted.

Landing, a primitive name for a primitive harbour or port. For instance, Port Arthur, on Lake Superior, was originally known as Prince Arthur's Landing; and Port Athabasca sounds more businesslike than Athabasca Landing.

Land knows, the Lord knows; a feminine form of protestation, as in the speech of a Western Martha who tarried by the wash-tub when the rest of the community was up at the depot to see a great man's train pass through, "He ain't nothing but a man—and, **land knows,** men is common enough, and ornery enough, without runnin' like a band of sheep to see one." Martha might have varied the expression with **Land sakes,** which, being interpreted, means For the Lord's sake.

Land-poor (adj.), a person who is unable to meet his payments on land.

Land shark, a person having large land interests or dealings.

Land-seekers, a general term applied to immigrants or new arrivals in search of land whereon to settle.

Land Titles Office, an important establishment in Canadian cities where records of all land transactions are kept and where settlers and homesteaders receive their certificates, patents or deeds for land they acquire.

Lariat, a lasso, a rope with a loop at one end, forming part of the equipment of a cowboy, and with which he is usually an expert in catching wild horses and cattle.

Larrigans, moccasins made from deer-hide; sometimes called **buckskin moccasins.** (See **Moccasins**).

Lasso, a lariat, a rope with a loop at one end, in use among the cowboys for catching wild horses and cattle. Also used as a verb.

Last Best West, a favourite term for describing a new district beyond which one must not dream of anything better.

Launder, to wash and iron. **Laundered,** the condition of clothes and linen newly-arrived from the laundry.

Lean-to, an outhouse attached to the main structure, usually a back-kitchen or a wood-shed.

Legislative Assembly, the official name of the parliaments of the provinces, except those of Quebec and Nova Scotia, which are officially known as Legislative Councils.

Legislature, the general name for the Parliament of a Province.

Lemme, pronounced either in one syllable or in two words, and meaning **let me. Gimme** is a word constructed on the same principle of contraction.

Lemon. Handed him a **lemon,** handed him something sour, as, for instance, a snub, a disappointment; discouragement when reward was expected. "Handed him a **raw onion**" is another way of expressing it.

Let-down, a reverse, a loss, a humiliation. The person so suffering may say he has had a severe **let-down,** and **let down on the face** may be supposed to mean still greater humiliation. "Think of me getting **let down on my face** like that, and by a woman," was the exclamation of a cowboy after meditating for a moment over a snubbing.

Lid, a hat, a cap. **Take your lid off,** take your hat off.

Limit, the extreme. He's the limit, he's past comprehension, or almost unendurable. But note that the emphasis is placed on the first word—"the" limit.

Line, advice, guidance. To get a line on any matter is to be told how to proceed in connection therewith or how the matter at present stands.

Liquor permit. In early days in the North-West Territories, when intoxicating liquors were prohibited, favored persons could, on application, obtain from the Governor a permit for a stated quantity of liquor.

Livery, properly a **livery-stable,** a place where horses are kept and let out for hire, or where horses are housed and boarded. **Livery** is the name such a place gets in the West.

Live wire, a hustler.

Loam, decayed vegetable matter, the most fertile of all soils.

Loan (noun), anything lent. **Loan** is also used as a verb; as, "I'll **loan** you a dollar," which dollar is then said to have been **loaned.**

Lode, a gold or any metallic vein in the ground or rock.

Lodger, a person who resides in the house, having both bed and board. (See **Boarder** and **Roomer**).

Log, the felled tree, after it has been denuded of branches and prepared for transportation to the lumber mill. The word is also used as a verb, to **log,** meaning to cut the felled timber into logs of the length required at the lumber mill or as its growth and shape will permit.

Log cabin, a hut constructed of logs laid one upon another, with the interstices blocked up with odd bits of lumber, earth, moss, plaster, etc.

Logger. In the West, **loggers** are those who make a special business of logging, selling the logs delivered to the mills, at so much per thousand feet.

Logging, the work of cutting the felled trees into logs, and of conveying it down the logging roads.

Logging road, the road on which logs are drawn from the standing timber to the river or lake landing.

Log-jammer, a derrick for loading logs on to sleighs or cars.

Lone-Star State, Texas, which has a single star in the centre of the flag. People of Texas are sometimes dubbed **Beefheads.**

Long shot, a hazardous guess.

Looking for trouble, making trouble; or, more correctly, inviting trouble or unpleasantness.

Loop, the cowboy's familiar way of talking of his lariat or lasso. (See **Lariat**).

Loosen up, words much used by the Canadian housewife in reference to the husband's purse strings. When additional funds are required for household or personal purposes, hubby is expected to **loosen up.** The words may be applied to the loosening if any purse, willingly or unwillingly, and a reluctant debtor may even be requested to **loosen up.**

Lot, the piece of land, from the front street to the back lane, upon which the town-dweller has his house.

Love-apple, an old-time name for the tomato.

Lumber, an Old-Country word, but purely American as now used, and denoting boards or planks. The new meaning originated at Boston, Mass., where the over-supplies of timber lying about the wharves were described as lumber, "lumbering up the wharf."

Lumber, timber, wood, in its unmanufactured or manufactured state.

Lumberman, a merchant who deals in timber, doors, sashes, etc., for building purposes. The **Lumberjack** is the man who has to face the elements and cut down the trees and prepare them for despatching to the timber mills or into the towns to be used as fuel. (See **Cordwood**).

Lumber dealer, known in Great Britain as a timber merchant, but in Canada and the States as one who deals in sawn boards, planking, shingles, lath, etc.

Lumberman, a lumber or timber merchant.

Lunkhead, a stupid person.

Lynch, to punish without the forms of law or trial, as sometimes practised by an American mob, who hang the miscreant to the nearest tree and then riddle his body with bullets. John Lynch, a Virginian farmer, who so acted, was the person whose name has become associated with this form of summary retribution.

M

Mackinaw, a heavy woollen cloth much in favour among lumberjacks. A lumberjack also speaks of his thick winter jacket as his **mackinaw.**

Mahogany overcoat, a coffin.

Mail, letters going or coming by post. Here's some **mail** for you, here are some letters for you. **Mail those letters,** post those letters.

Mail clerk, a post-office sorter, or clerk in the mail room of an ocean liner, the person who looks after the postal arrangements in a large hotel.

Mail order, an order for goods to be sent by post or express service. **Mail order house,** a business establishment or a special department in a large departmental store which advertises freely and does trade through the post or express service. (See **Express**).

Make good. (See **Good**).

Manitoba, the most easterly of the three Prairie Provinces. Winnipeg the capital and the largest city in Canada west of Lake Superior, is about midway between the Atlantic and Pacific Oceans. Emerging out of the Red River Settlement, later known as the colony of Assiniboia, Manitoba as a Province took its name from Lake Manitoba, the islands of which were believed by the natives to be the habitation of the Manito, or Great Spirit.

Maple, a tree of great sentimental value to Canadians. It comes of the soapberry family and embraces many kinds, some of which furnish valuable lumber for carpentry and cabinet work, and one, acer saccharinum, yields the maple syrup and maple sugar of commerce.

Masher, a dude, a fop, a would-be lady-killer.

Maverick, a cow that is running free without an owner; an unbranded steer.

Meal tickets may be purchased in most of the cafes and boarding houses, and these provide twenty-one meals at the price of twenty. Each ticket shows twenty-one small squares, and, instead of paying cash for each meal, the boarder has a hole punched in one of these squares. "Speaking of hard luck," remarked United States Senator Klutch, "I had some hard luck once during my early days. I had just invested my last five dollars in a meal ticket, and as I started down the street a gust of wind tore the ticket from my hand. A lumberjack was passing, wearing heavy, hobnailed boots, and he stepped on my ticket and punched out four dollars eighty-five!"

Meat market, or **Meat store,** a butcher's shop, the latter term being applied to the slightly better-class establishments.

Medicine, a punishment, deserved or undeserved, or some unpleasant experience which one has to accept. Such things as a prisoner's sentence, an employer's reprimand, a curtain lecture, a husband's ill-treatment, etc., are described as a person's medicine, and the chronicler may add that "the patient took his medicine meekly."

Medicine man, an Indian to whom the members of the tribe go for cures for all diseases, mental, moral and physical. He also professes to exorcise evil spirits by magic.

Melon-cutting is the dividing up of extra company profits; the process by which directors and officials enrich themselves at the expense of the shareholders and the public.

Mem., Memo. or Memorandum, a note, a reminder. **Memoranda** (plural), several notes or a collection of notes.

Mennonites, a religious body of immigrants who live in communities, and whose creed is a curious mixture of Socialism and Individualism.

Merger, combine or union of two or more business concerns; also used as a verb, as "We propose to **merger** the whole cement trade."

Mess-house, the hut where lumbermen eat.

Metis, the offspring of French-Canadian and Indian parentage.

Militia, the army of Canada, which is an organisation somewhat similar to the Volunteers of the Old-Country. A permanent staff controls the militia, and there is also a small permanent force of artillery and Strathcona's Horse, the latter stationed at Winnipeg.

Mill, the tenth of a cent, a calculation used in the assessing of rates and taxes

Milling, the industry of converting the wheat into flour. A **milling plant** is what the newcomer has hitherto known as a flour mill.

Missouri. "I'm from Missouri, equivalent to saying "I want to know the reason why," which is alleged to be a characteristic of immigrants from that State. The people of the State of Missouri are also known as **Pukes.**

Mitts, big winter or working gloves with a stall for the thumb and a single compartment for the four fingers. When they reach well up the forearm, above the coat sleeve, they are described as gauntlets.

Mixed farming, growing or raising a large variety of things on the farm. Its practice is becoming more common on the principle of "Don't put all your eggs in one basket."

Mixer, a man who gets among company, who makes himself popular. To make a business hum, a firm sometimes advertises for a good **mixer.** On the other hand, some employers aver that the man with a reputation as a **good mixer** hasn't got time to attend to the regular job.

Mix-up, a fight.

Moccasins, a general term for various styles of footwear, all in imitation of the original moccasins of the Indians, the essential idea being that the sole, the lower part of the sides, and the heel and toe are in one piece, there being no hard sole or raised heel. They are made from various materials, such as pig-skin, horse-hide, etc., and are used with extra pairs of socks or stockings. (See **Indian moccasins, Larrigans,** and **Shoepacks**).

Molasses, sugar syrup, treacle.

Money. For rough or approximate calculations, the Canadian cent may be reckoned as equal to the British halfpenny; the quarter, or 25-cent piece, as one shilling; a dollar as four shillings; two-and-a-half dollars as ten shillings; and five dollars as one pound and sixpence.

Money to burn, an abundance of ready cash. A Member of the Dominion House of Commons stated that the farmers of the West had **money to burn,** meaning thereby that they had all they needed and some over. **Money to throw at the birds** is a variation of the phrase.

Monolingual (adj.), in one language, or possessing the command of only one language. In the educational system of Canada, a **monolingual** school is one in which English is the language of both teachers and scholars. (See **Bilingual**).

Moose, the largest of the deer species of animals, growing sometimes to the height of 17 hands and attaining a weight of 1,200 pounds. "It has palmated horns, with a short, thick neck, and an upright mane of a light brown colour. The eyes are small, the ears a foot long, very broad and slouching; the upper lip is square and hangs over the lower one. The European variety of the moose is known as the elk."

Mortgage (noun), the temporary pledge of property as security for the payment of a debt or loan. **Mortgage** (verb), to pawn property as security for the debt. The document itself is also spoken of as the **mortgage.**

Mortgagee, the person to whom property is mortgaged; the person who has advanced the loan and who holds the property in pawn.

Mortgager, a person who borrows money and puts his property into pawn as security for the debt.

Mosey, (or **Moosey**), to poke around ferreting out information.

Mosquito, a gnat-like insect, having, in the female, a black proboscis which pierces the flesh of men and animals, and which also forms a syphon through which the blood flows. They are commonly known as **skeeters,** and to keep them out of the houses in the hot summer days screen doors and screen windows are fitted up, thus allowing the ordinary doors and windows to remain open.

Mossback, a slow-moving individual from the country. "A rolling stone gathers no moss;" the **mossback** is the other fellow.

Most, also used in the same sense as almost; as, **I'm most starved,** or **I'm most frozen.**

Mouth. Working his mouth, talking much and saying little.

Move. Get a move on, get busy, make a start, look lively.

Movie, a moving picture show.

M.P., member of the Dominion Parliament at Ottawa. **M.P.P.,** member of a Provincial Parliament; or, sometimes, **M.L.A.,** member of the Provincial Legislative Assembly.

Mucilage. One must not speak of gum in Canada; it is always mucilage. (See **Chewing gum**).

Mud, land, real estate. A Canadian publication has "Money and Mud" as a heading for its financial and real estate page.

Mudcat State, Mississippi.

Municipality, a rural district, village, town or city which has been incorporated and has a government or council. Generally, however, by a municipality an incorporated rural municipality is referred to.

Muskeg, a piece of marshy land; or what would be called marsh or bogland in the Old-Country.

Musk-ox, a hollow-horned ruminant, belonging to the Arctic regions, which combines some of the characteristics of the sheep and the ox. "Both sexes are horned, the large horns being united at the skull, but deflected downward at each side of the head. Its hair is long, fine and brown, shaggy about the neck and shoulders, with yellowish wool beneath. The limbs are stout and short. It exhales a musky effluvium, whence its name."

Muskrat, found in great numbers wherever there is water. This animal is an important fur-bearer, two millions of its skins (representing the capture of the entire North-West) being shipped to London every year by the Hudson's Bay Company.

Mustang, a horse descendant of Spanish stock introduced into America in the sixteenth century; the former wild horse of the Far West, now practically domesticated.

Mutt, which being interpreted means, a chump.

My! a feminine exclamation equivalent to the **Oh!** of the Old-Country. "**My,** but don't these flowers smell awful sweet!"

N

National Park (The Canadian), a national reservation of 5732 square miles, embracing parts of the valleys of the Bow, Spray and Cascade Rivers, Lake Minnewanka and several mountain ranges, and beyond the "Divide," the Yoho Valley, and the country to the west and south of it, is the largest park in the world, being nearly half as large again as the famous Yellowstone Park in the United States. Banff, on the C.P.R., is the most convenient railway station.

Naturalization. A British subject qualifies for a vote after he has been one year in Canada and a resident for three months in the constituency in which he claims a vote. A foreign immigrant may neutralize as a Canadian after three years' residence in the Dominion.

Nearby, near bye, close to, adjacent.

Neck. In the neck, in a vulnerable spot, or in a vital spot. After the prairie fire, and the forage had all been consumed, the rancher remarked to the cowboy, "After this fire, the cattle are the ones to get it in the neck this winter," meaning thereby that the cattle were to be the greatest sufferers.

Never-again club, a purely imaginary confraternity, the members of which are supposed to have taken a solemn oath never to touch intoxicants again. These usually announce their membership when feeling the effects of a long spree.

New Caledonia, previously the name of the mainland of British Columbia.

New chum, a new arrival, a new-comer, an expression mostly used in the mining camps.

New-comer, a new arrival in the country.

New Manitoba. In 1912 the Province was extended northwest to the 60th parallel and eastward to a line drawn from the northeast angle to the original boundaries of the Province to the most northeasterly portion of Island Lake, thence northeast to intersect the southern shores of Hudson Bay in longitude 89 degrees. This district is 178,000 sq. miles, i.e., over 4,000 sq. miles larger than the old Province of Manitoba. The new district contains Port Nelson and Fort Churchill, the only two "ports" of Hudson Bay. This territory is practically unexplored.

Newsie, generally a street newspaper seller, but the vendors of papers, books, cigars, etc., on trains are also known as **Newsies.**

News-print, the technical name for the paper used in the production of a newspaper or the cheapest kinds of printing jobs.

Next! a jocular intimation that your story is a lie. **Next!** is an invitation for you to try again.

Nickel, a 5-cent piece.

Nickel. (See **Three for a nickel**).

Nifty, neat, natty, tidy, smart.

Nigger, a negro. New-comers should note negroes and Indians are two very distinct and different races.

Nigger in the fence, or **Nigger in the wood-pile,** some suspicious circumstance. **There's a nigger in the fence** is the usual exclamation on the first discovery of crooked doings and when the matter must be probed. One can easily imagine that the phrase had its origin in the States, where, if some barnyard depredations were discovered, a nigger was the likeliest culprit, and the said nigger was most likely to be in hiding near bye, or in the fence.

Nigger in the melon-patch, a phrase better known in the States, and having the same meaning as **nigger in the fence.**

Nigger in the wood-pile. (See **Nigger in the fence**).

Nope, no.

Northland (The), the name which poets and writers of romance have bestowed on the lands lying between the Last Best West and the Arctic Circle. Robert W. Service, the Canadian poet, has shed a glamour of romance over this region.

North-West Fur Company, a hustling Montreal concern which, after a fur trade war and a fort-building competition unique in the annals of the Dominion, was absorbed by the Hudson's Bay Company, but which is credited with having started the progressive movement in Canada as far as fur-trading and Empire-building in the West are concerned.

North-West Territories comprise all British territories in North America and all islands adjacent thereto not included within any province or the Yukon Territory and the colony of Newfoundland.

Nosing around, seeking information, or poking one's nose into other people's business.

Nothin' doin', an expression that has become a by-word. Though originally it was a boss's reply to applicants when he had no work to offer them, it has come to be a frequent reply to an applicant for alms, to a drummer for whom there is no order, to a suitor whose attentions are not desired, or to anyone who is not to be granted what they desire. It has become a denial and a refusal in all sorts of circumstances, and even if you tell your choicest story, an unappreciative listener may mutter "nothin' doin'" and pass on. He means that there's **nothin' doin'** in the smiling line.

Nothing to it, nothing in it, nothing attached to it; words that may be uttered in reference to some story or scheme that is not worth consideration.

Notions, smallwares, haberdashery. The notions counter is a popular department of the large stores.

Not too bad, a characteristic Canadian reply to an inquiry regarding one's health or circumstances. Literally it means, "Oh, about fair," or "Can't complain."

Notation, a footnote or memorandum, a remembrancer. A word mostly used in business.

No use for it, want to have nothing to do with it, done with it. The words are also used in reference to individuals. In throwing over an old or undesirable acquaintance, a Canadian will say, "I've no use for him."

Nowhere, not in the reckoning, or so far behind as not to be worth counting.

Nugget, a lump of metal, especially of native gold.

Nutty, batty, dippy, wrong in the head.

O

Office, the business department of an hotel, usually just inside the main entrance, where visitors, or **guests,** as they are called, **register** their names on arrival. **Office** is also the word used to indicate a doctor's consulting room or surgery, and (what appears to the newcomer as quite unprofessional) the **doctor's office** may be found in the same building as barristers, solicitors, real estate agents, contractors, etc.

Ogloo. (See **Igloo**).

Oil. To **strike oil** (or **ile**), to meet with a stroke of good luck.

O.K., signifying that the documents or printed matter on which the letters have been written are **Oll Korrect**, i.e., all correct. This is an Americanism, and said to have been originally marked on an important document by a high-standing official to signify that all was right and proper.

Old, an adjective frequently used by the easy-going or good-natured Canadian. He will say, "Any old thing will do for me," "Give me any old thing for dinner," "Any old place will make a bedroom for me." In a different humour he might say, "Any old thing (or story, or lie) won't do for me."

Old Glory, a pet name for the Stars and Stripes, the flag of the United States.

Old-head, an old man. In a discussion, the wise guys and the elderly men in the company may be addressed as **old-heads.**

Old man, the chief, the boss. The head of an establishment, if he is elderly, is referred to by his subordinates as the **Old man.**

Old skate, an old person or thing of little use.

Old-timer, actually an early settler or old citizen, but the ingratiating bum will often salute the new-comer as old-timer, when the drinks are on the new-comer every time.

One best bet. (See **Best bet**).

One on him. (See **Put one over on him**).

On the side. (See **Side line**).

Onto, a combination of the words **on** and **to,** used in such a sentence as "He put all the blame **onto** the others." It is argued that **onto** is as permissible as **into**, and it is upto us to agree.

Opium joint, an opium den.

Option. To obtain an option on a given piece of property, a cash deposit is made, according to arrangement with the owner, who agrees not to sell said property in the time specified by the option. At the expiration date, the holder of the option either purchases the property, applying the deposit on the purchase price, or lets it go, in which case he sacrifices his deposit. Speculators who have reason to believe certain property will have a quick rise in value, frequently obtain an option for thirty or sixty days, and complete a sale at a greatly advanced price, to some other individual, before their option expires. That is, A gets an option from B, and sells the property to C, after which A squares up accounts with B and pockets his profit without having actually taken possession of the property.

O.T., when chalked opposite a train number on a depot time-board, means that the incoming train is **on time,** or running according to schedule. **On time,** when referring to an individual, may mean that he is always prompt or on hand when he is wanted.

Outfit. Some Canadians will use anything but the proper name for an object, so outfit sometimes fits in when speaking of a house, store, cafe, or even an individual.

Out-hoof, out-run. "Max was a sport from 'way back. He travelled with a swift bunch, but, swift though they were, none of them could **out-hoof** Mr. Max when it came right down to pure recklessness."

Out of business, a sporting phrase which, used in reference to the knock-out blow, means that one of the fighters is out of the game; or it may be used in other walks of life, as, for instance, when a certain high official became "inebriated with the exuberance of his own verbosity" and divulged too much to the reporters, he was informed by his chief that such blank dash foolishness was enough to put any Government **out of business.**

Out of sight may be given as a reply to an inquiry as to the state of one's health, suggesting that the person is in such good form that he could leap up into the clouds, out of sight. A story is told of a Scotsman who heard the reply for the first time, and determined to work it off at the earliest opportunity. He, however, met too suddenly an Irish friend, who asked after his health, and the nearest he could get to the Canadian reply was, "Oh, I can't be seen." The Irishman marvelled at the new-found Canadianism, and in his turn tried to store it up for the first favourable opportunity. But his memory was as defective as that of the Scotsman, and when next a friend asked him about the condition of his health all that he could remember by way of reply was, "Och, be jabers, Oi'm hidin'!"

Outside lots, a term used in the real estate business to indicate lots beyond the city limits. (See **Inside lots**).

Overalls, or jumpers, rough canvas trousers which reach well up the chest and back and are fastened over the shoulders with attached braces, used by outdoor workers and those doing rough or dirty work in the warehouses and factories. A Canadian idea worth copying in the Old-Country.

Overshoes, rubber shoes with felt uppers, worn over the ordinary leather boots. They keep the feet warm and also prevent slipping on the ice. (See **Rubbers**).

P

Pack ice, ice in a broken, floating body.

Pack train, a string of mules or horses conveying, on their backs, food or supplies across country where wheels or sleds are impossible.

Pan-handle, to beg, to importune, to persistently molest or accost people for help, money, or drink. **Pan-handler,** a beggar, a flagrant mendicant.

Panhandle State, West Virginia.

Panned out. Panned out well, showed good results; panned out badly, something that worked out as a failure.

Pannikin, a little mug or a small pan.

Papoose, a child (Indian).

Pard, a partner, a chum; a word reminiscent of the gold-mining camps.

Park country, where the prairie is dotted with bluffs. (See **Bluff**).

Passed on, adjudicated upon, dealt with, or disposed of; a phrase used in reference to questions discussed or business transacted at a business meeting.

Passed up, an expression borrowed from the gambling table and signifying that the person or article in question is not wanted. When the impetuous cowboy had prepared a meal for a lady he had succoured from the storm, and found that she did not dig into the pork and beans with great gusto, he pressed her by remarking, "I'm liable to feel insulted if you **pass up** my cooking this way." Sometimes, also, it has the same meaning as **turned down,** as when the portly hostess declared to the fair young debutante, "I'm real glad you took a hold and danced as you did, and never **passed nobody up,** like some would a done. Even danced with Polycarp Jenks—and there ain't hardly any woman but what'll **turn him down.**"

Patch, a portion, section, or slice of a field devoted to the growth of certain vegetables. Thus, we hear of the **cabbage patch,** the **potato patch,** the **tomato patch,** etc.

Patrol, a policeman on street duty. **Patrol wagon,** police wagon or automobile, in place of the Old-Country's Black Maria.

Paupers, as known in the Old-Country, are unknown in the West. There are many charitable societies to help the really deserving poor, but no workhouses to harbour the loafers and won't-works.

Pavement, the paved or asphalted roadway for vehicular traffic. That part of the street known in the Old-Country as the **pavement** is called the **sidewalk** in Canada. (See **Sidewalk**).

Pay-streak, in mining parlance is a seam of gold; though any good-paying proposition may 'also be called a **pay-streak.**

Peanuts, popular among Canadian youths when roasted or made up with pop-corn or candy, or **as a** relish, food, or confection. **Peanut politics,** petty politics, especially when of a vindictive or personal nature.

Peavey, a staff-like tool used by lumberjack river drivers in moving the logs.

P. D. Q. "Get out of here P. D. Q. is an order that should not be trifled with." (See **R. L. H.**).

Pecker. The innocent Old-Country expression, "Keep your pecker up," must never be used in Canada, where it has a very vulgar meaning.

Peeled. Keep your eyes peeled, keep your eyes open, be on the watch, don't go to sleep.

Peg. Occasionally Winnipeg is spoken of as the **Peg.**

Peg, a drink of intoxicants. "Will you have a peg?" is how they put it.

Peigans, a tribe of Indians.

Pelican State, Louisiana, where pelicans are common.

Pelt, the skin of a beast with the hair on it; a raw hide.

Pemican, buffalo meat cooked and preserved in the fat of the buffalo.

Pen, a penitentiary, a prison.

Penitentiary, a gaol.

Permit, permission, or a license. In the building trade, a permit is required before constructing.

Pesky, annoying, troublesome, vexatious.

Peter, as in the phrase **peter out,** is to work out, dwindle away, or disappear. Gold miners are the most frequent users of the phrase, using it in reference to a vein or lode that has worked out or has been lost. "The wind of one of the fighters **petered out**" is a sentence that may be found in an account of a boxing contest.

Philadelphia lawyer, a limb of the law alleged to be the very essence of cuteness. "Enough to puzzle a Philadelphia lawyer" is equivalent to saying that the matter under discussion is enough to puzzle the sharpest man in the world.

Picayune, paltry, mean, small; **as, picayune politicians,** men who have no standing in the parties.

Pickaback, or Pickapack, on the back in the manner of a pack, as a child is sometimes carried.

Pickaninny, a young child is thus styled by the negroes in the Southern States. The word is now completely naturalized in Canada.

Pickled, intoxicated; has a swell "bun" on.

Pigeon (or Pidgin) English, the jargon used for intercourse between the Chinese immigrants and the English-speaking races.

Pigeon's milk, an imaginary fluid for which boys and simpletons are frequently sent on the 1st of April.

Pike, a scared person, one afraid to risk his money, an invertebrate.

Piker, one who hits the pike (or highway) and hikes out of the town. Probably the latter word comes from England, the land of turnpikes, which are, as yet, almost unknown in Western Canada.

Pike-pole, the pole used by rivermen to keep the logs on their straight course down the river. It is fitted with a sharp point at one end.

Pile, a fortune made by an individual, and of just that amount which satisfies his ambitions or permits him to take a house in Easy Street.

Pilferage, theft of goods in transit, or leakage by petty pilfering.

Pimp; an abandoned, depraved creature who lives on the immoral earnings of unfortunate women and who is usually on hand to blackmail the woman's followers, or even the woman herself. Canadian police officials have little mercy for these ghouls.

Pinch, steal; and a person who has been arrested for some minor offence may be said to have been **pinched.**

Pine-tree State, Maine, where there are extensive pine forests. Maine is also known as the **Lumber State.**

Pioneer, a leader in a new enterprise, a man who opens up a new section of country, who goes out into the wilds to spread civilization.

Pips, the marks, no matter of what suit, on playing cards. The ace card is sometimes called a single pip.

Placer gold, surface gold that is washed by hand.

Plains, a general term now coming into use, and indicating the wide stretches of cultivated level land in the Provinces of Manitoba, Saskatchewan and Alberta, where, according to the boosting literature or the real estate agents, one may find "an uninterrupted view to the distant horizon," a valuable asset for which no extra charge is made.

Plant, a manufacturing outfit or machinery.

Plat (v.), to survey and subdivide land into lots.

Platform, the principles of a candidate or a party at election time. Each principle is called a **plank.**

Playfest, a feast of play or sports, a gala, a tournament.

Plow, the Canadian and American way of spelling **Plough.**

Plug, a square or cake of tobacco.

Plug (verb), to put a plug (a bullet) into a man; or, to give a man a staggering blow.

Plug, the patient, willing, steady-working old horse; the animal that wouldn't know what to do if put into a green field for a week's holiday. The word is also frequently applied to a steady-going, industrious individual, and of such someone has written: "Pin your faith to the plug who keeps eternally at it; the fellow who gets up every morning and does so much, and is ready to do it again next day. He lays up more shining dollars in the bank than the swift sport who lays around all summer waiting for luck to come along and turn a stream of silver into his pocket. One cackling Plymouth Rock hen is worth a dozen screaming eagles when it comes to paying off the mortgage. The plug is the fellow who steadies the ship and acts as ballast when the boat begins to rock. The plug is the fellow who lives contentedly and long, and when he passes away the local paper says, 'He leaves his family in comfortable circumstnaces.' "

Plug hat, a high hat, a silk hat.

Plumb, an innocent swear-word that is in use amongst the best type of manhood in the camps and on the prairie; as, "Plumb ashamed of myself," "My elbow's pumb getting a cramp in it," "If she wasn't so plumb innocent," the general meaning of the word, apparently, being **downright.**

Plunk, a dollar. Two plunks, two dollars, and so on.

Plunk, a word used in much the same sense as **plump** and **plant** in the Old-Country in reference to money; as, **Plunk your money down,** or **He plunked his money down.** "When the Reverend Baltimore Criddle first **plunked** his heavy foot upon one end of Washington street, all the negroes wondered why the other end didn't tip up."

Plurality, a majority, a word much used at election times.

Plute, a plutocrat, a man who has made his pile and has become a power in the land.

Poison, drink. **Nominate your poison,** name your drink.

Police magistrate, a stipendiary.

Pollywog, a frog or a tadpole.

Pony jacket, a woman's winter coat made of pony cloth, or what is called Russian pony, a fur said to be cowskin.

Poorhouse. None in Western Canada. (See **Pauper**).

Porkopolis, Chicago.

Portage, a break in a line of water-communication over which boats, goods, etc., must be carried by land, as from one lake to another, or along the banks of rivers at a point where there are rapids or a waterfall. The word is also used as a verb, an instance of such use being found in Robert W. Service's Ballad of the Northern Lights, "We poled and lined up nameless streams, **portaged** o'er hill and plain; We burned our boat to save the nails, and built our boat again."

Posse, any hastily-collected body of men; a **posse of policemen** being a squad of the force collected for some special duty.

Postcards sent to correspondents in Canada or the United States require only a one-cent stamp. Postcards for Great Britain, Newfoundland, and countries in the Postal Union require a two-cent stamp, as in the case of a letter.

Pot-hole, a deceptive water-filled hole frequently found in the lumber woods and on the prairie.

Pound, the place in which stray horses, cattle, etc., are housed until claimed or sold by the authorities.

Pow-wow (n.), an Indian council talk, generally accompanied by much dignified ceremony, smoking the calumet, or pipe of peace, and speeches by the chiefs. A pow-wow may be held by one tribe or representatives of several tribes, or by Indians and white men. The word is also used in a colloquial sense, to mean a business talk or discussion, as, "We had quite a pow-wow over the matter."

Prairie, an extensive tract of flat or rolling land, covered 'with tall grass or brushwood, and practically destitute of trees.

Prairie antelope, the pronghorn which inhabits the western parts of North America, frequenting the plains in summer and the mountains in winter, and is sometimes called the Rocky Mountain antelope. It is one of the few hollow-horned ruminants and the only living one in which the horny branch is sheathed.

Prairie chicken, a bird of the grouse species. Also known as the **prairie hen, prairie fowl, prairie grouse.**

Prairie dew, whiskey, or mountain dew.

Prairie dog. (See **Coyote**).

Prairie madness, the melancholia which attacks the lonely homesteader.

Prairie oyster (or **cocktail**), a raw yolk dropped into spirits.

Prairie Province, a name that belonged exclusively to Manitoba up till 1905, when Alberta and Saskatchewan, having received Provincial autonomy, also shared in the title with it. Thus there are now three Prairie Provinces.

Prairie schooner, an immigrant covered-in wagon or cart, in which, in the old days, long journeys were made across Western Canada.

Prairie State, Illinois.

Prayer-book, a pack of cards.

Preaching-shop, a church or chapel.

Pre-emption, the act or right of purchasing before others. In certain districts a homesteader may pre-empt a quarter-section alongside his homestead at a cheap rate. (See **Homesteader**).

Print shop, a small printing office, though usually better equipped than the **cock-robin shops** of the Old-Country.

Probe (verb), to inquire, to examine, to investigate. **Probe** (noun), an inquiry, an investigation. **Probe** is apparently the correct word to use when referring to a searching inquiry into some irregularity or supposed fraud.

Prod. On the prod, in a "contrairy" humour, in a bad temper, disposed to prod people into a similar frame of mind.

Proposition, a favourite word in Canada to describe a business undertaking or a new scheme. The newcomer who has an abundance of cash is soon waylaid by agents who can put a first-class business **proposition** in his way. "A dandy **proposition**" is a common description.

Prospect (with the accent on the latter syllable), to look for, to explore. **Prospector,** a man who searches new country for a homestead, for gold, for lumber, or on account of new railways or any other enterprise.

Proven, proved, a survival of the Scotch form of the word.

Publicity Commissioner, chief advertising agent, or chief booster. The Dominion Government, each of the Provincial Governments, and most of the cities, towns, railway companies and live business enterprises have a Publicity Commissioner, who looks after the advertising and supplies information to inquirers.

Puck, the hard rubber disc used in the game of hockey in place of a ball.

Puck-chaser, a hockey player.

Pull, power, advantage, hold. To have a **pull** on a person is to have some power or influence over him. A minister who attracted a large congregation was said to have a **pulling manner,** a well-dressed store window was said to be a good **puller,** and a well-constructed advertisement was said to have great **pulling qualities.**

Pullman, or **Pullman car,** first-class travelling accommodation on a railway train. The lower class is the **tourist car** and the lowest class is the **colonist car.** (See **Pullman and Colonist**).

Pull off, take place; **Pulled off,** took place; as, "the fight which they expected to **pull off** last night will be **pulled off** to-night."

Pull out. A train does not "start" or "leave;" it pulls out. Thus a person may say, "I **pull out** at 4.45," and when inquiring as to the time of departure of a train, the inquirer is told that it **"pulls out"** at a certain time.

Pulp, minced timber, or timber that has been sawn and pounded into dust, with sufficient moisture added to hold it together. Further treatment at the paper-mill reduces it to a liquid state, and it is then manufactured into paper.

Pumpkin, a kind of melon, and with much of the shape of a melon, but with depressed ends. It is, in some parts, much used as food, prepared in a variety of ways, as in the favourite pumpkin-pie, and also fed to stock where it is over-plentiful. **Pun-kin** is the general pronunciation.

Pumpkin, an immigrant from Boston, so named from the abundance of pumpkins raised and eaten in that part of the States.

Pump-sucker, a water drinker, or teetotaller.

Punk, old, stale, poor, insipid.

Push, a foreman, a leading hand, the man who pushes the work along. **Head push,** the head foreman, or manager.

Puts on no dog, puts on no airs, puts on no side.

Put one over on him, catching him with the latest puzzling by-word or smart saying, giving him a Roland for his Oliver, giving him the worst of it, caught him napping. A Winnipeg newspaper recently put up the heading, "Put one over on Bernard Shaw," and under it had the following story: "There is at least one woman in the United Kingdom with the reputation of having on an occasion gone Bernard Shaw one better. This particular lady had sent Shaw an invitation to dinner. The reply she received was this: 'Don't you know that I don't accept dinner invitations from ladies?' A few days later Shaw obtained his answer. 'The invitation you received was a mistake. Don't you know, Mr. Shaw, that I issue invitations to gentlemen only?'"

Q

Quaker City, Philadelphia, so called from the fact that William Penn, its founder, belonged to the Society of Friends.

Quaker's bargain, a Yea or Nay transaction, take it or leave it.

Quantum, as much as you want or ought to have. **Quantum suff.,** enough.

Quarter, 25-cent piece, quarter of a dollar. The quarter-dollar bill, now rarely seen, is known as a **Shinplaster.**

Quarter section, 160 acres, more or less, the portion of land granted to the homesteader. (See **Homestead**).

Queen City of Canada, Toronto.

Queen City of the Lakes, Buffalo.

Queen City of the Mississippi, St. Louis.

Queer the game, upset the game, spoil it, make it a farce or a fraud. A person who **queers** himself with his associates is one who has made himself unpopular or has raised doubts as to his sanity.

Quencher, a drink. Also **Modest quencher,** anything short of a big drink, and frequently the beginning of a big drunk.

Quick and nimble, a jeering reference to leisurely movement; more like a bear than a squirrel.

Quiet, to appease, to settle. Thus a payment may be made to **quiet** a claim or an appeal may be made to the Legislature to **quiet** (or settle) the title to land the possession of which has been long in dispute.

Quill-driver, a penman, an author or a journalist. **Hero of the quill,** a distinguished writer.

Quirt, a cowboy's whip, usually having a heavily-loaded handle which makes it "very awkward for the coo."

Quitter, a man who does not remain long on one job, one who is frequently changing. (See **Sticker**).

R

Racket, confusion, disorder, clamour, or noisy merriment.

Racoon, an animal about the size of a small fox, the greyish-brown fur of which is used for the make-up of coats and hats.

Radiator, the neatly-arranged (and usually brightly-painted) cluster of metal tubes which forms part of the furnishing of rooms in steam-heated houses.

Raft, lumber strongly braced up to float in one mass down a river. Rafts on Canadian waterways are sometimes of enormous size.

Rafter, or **Raftsman,** a worker on the lumber rafts, assembling the logs and navigating them downstream to the lumber mills.

Rag, a newspaper, as described by its opponents or supporters of the opposing organ.

Ragtime music, gay lightsome music of the cake-walk style, or common music, as contradistinguished from classic music.

Rail-bird, a hanger-on at a race track.

Railroad, to drive, to jam through, to get rid of in a hurry. At a recent trial in Canada it was said that there was a plot to **railroad** a certain individual into the insane asylum.

Rainy day, hard times; whence **to lay up for a rainy day,** to provide against bad times.

Raise, to rear children, crops, cattle, etc. **Raise Cain,** to create trouble or a rumpus.

Raise dog, an expression alleged to be used by women, and which signifies that they will raise all the snapping and snarling possible.

Rake-off, a scoop-in; the amount the agent receives, and retains, above the price agreed to by the seller.

Ranch, a farm or range (originally **Rancho**), on which horses, cattle, and all kinds of livestock, even chickens, are reared. A chicken ranch, when located near a city, is quite a profitable proposition. The immense horse and cattle ranches (or ranges) of the Far West still, however, form one of the picturesque features of Canadian enterprise.

Rancher, or **Ranchman,** owner or manager of a ranch.

Range. (See **Ranch**).

Rapids, the quick-waters or fast-flowing portion of a river, that portion where the river races to a waterfall. (See **Shooting the rapids**).

Rastle, to strive, to struggle, to fight.

Rat, a blackleg, a scab, a man accepting less than the trade-union scale of pay or working when his mates have struck.

Rather, an emphatic affirmative; Yes, I should say so.

Rattle, to confuse, to harass or worry a nervous person in the performance of a difficult game or duty.

Rattled, bothered, confused, disconcerted, all balled-up. (See **Balled-up**).

Raw, annoyed, sore, mad about something that has happened.

Raw deal, a bare-faced swindle.

Razorbacks, a species of hogs, having sharp backs. Humorists allege that razorbacks saw or cut the boards when they pass through a low-roofed enclosure.

Reader, a newspaper advertisement done up in the form of a paragraph or article and placed in the news columns, the advertiser paying special rates.

Real estate, land, sometimes called mud. **Real estate agent,** a land agent.

Reckon. (See **I guess**).

Red, a cent, a coin. **Not a red,** without a cent; and the person who declares that he has **not a red** may either mean that he has no money with him or that he is **stoney broke.**

Red, familiar curtailed name of the Red River.

Red Indian, or **Redskin,** an Indian, so called because of the tinge of red in his complexion.

Red Light District, that part of a Canadian city in which immorality abounds; also known as the **cluster** or **hookshops.**

Red River cart, a primitive vehicle much used in the early days of settlement in the West. It was constructed entirely of wood, even to the wheels and axles, and, on the trail, emitted a screeching noise that was heard (so old-timers say) long before the cart itself came into sight.

Red River Settlement. (See **Settlement**).

Re-directed letters do not require any additional postage if re-directed and handed back to the mail-carrier or postman at the time of delivery or as soon thereafter as possible, unless, of course, it is re-directed to a place or country where a higher rate of postage is charged.

Reeve, the chief official in a rural municipality or in a village, a dignity akin to mayor.

Regardless, a single word that is used to indicate that a person or an undertaking is got up regardless of cost.

Regina, formerly the territorial capital and now the capital of the Province of Saskatchewan.

Register. When a visitor, or **guest,** as he is called, enters his name in the **register book** of an hotel, he is said to have **registered**

Remittance man, "a duke's son, a cook's son, or son of a belted earl," who "left his country for his country's good," and who receives regular remittances from home conditional on his keeping away from home. It is alleged that there are many such individuals in Western cities, and a stigma is attached to a person suspected of being a remittance man.

Repeater, a person who repeats some action over and over again. Thus the individual who appears frequently before the police magistrate is a repeater, and the man who appears in all contribution lists may be called a repeater. At election times, a man hired by the political bosses to record a vote, under different names, in different wards, is also a repeater. During an election a bunch of trained repeaters marched into a certain polling place. "What name?" inquired the election clerk of the leader, who was red-haired and freckled, and had a black eye. The voter glanced down at a slip of paper in his hand. "Isadore Mendelheim," he said. "That's not your real name and you know it!" said a suspicious challenger for a reform ticket. "It is me name," said the repeater, "and I'm goin' to vote under it—see?" Then from down the line came a voice: "Don't let that guy bluff you, Casey. Soitenly your name is Mendelheim!"

Riel (Louis), a French half-breed, leader of the Red River Rebellion of 1869-70. After that episode he was permitted to escape to the States, but returned to Canada to take part in the rising in Saskatchewan in 1885. He was executed at Regina on November 16, 1885.

Replevin (n.), an action to recover property that is alleged to have been wrongfully seized, on security being given to try the case.

Replevy (v.), to take back property wrongfully seized and giving security to try the right to it at law.

Riding a hunch. (See **Hunch**).

Rig, a horse and trap, a horse and sleigh; a word commonly applied to any vehicle that does light freight or parcel delivery work.

Right is one of the words which frequently finds a place in conversation and suggests right on the spot, as

Right here, Right there, Right now, Right away, etc.

Right-of-way, the strip of land along which the railroad stretches.

Ripsaw, a carpenter's handsaw, about 30 inches long, having three to three and one-half teeth per inch, and used for sawing or ripping down with the grain only.

River driver, a man who drives or steers logs down a river.

Rivermen, in the lumber trade, are those who look after the **drive,** or who steer the logs to the lumber mill, and generally doing all work on the river.

R.L.H., letters that are sometimes marked on a "rush" order to indicate the speed at which the order must be attended to. Their meaning is generally understood.

R.N.W.M.P., Royal North - West Mounted Police, the semi-military body of men who have charge of the outposts of empire in North-Western Canada. Once it was written, and once it was perfectly true, "The aristocratic ne'er-do-well frequently finds his way into the ranks of the Royal North-West Mounted Police."

Road-agents, stage robbers, or highwaymen; desperadoes of the early days of the American West.

Roast, to expose, to abuse, to rate, to tell a person off. A **roasting,** a severe rating or castigation in a speech.

Robe, an immense rug used when driving or sleighing, usually made of buffalo or similar skin.

Rockies, the Rocky Mountains, the famous range which stretches from north to south of British Columbia and down through some of the Western States.

Roll, or **Wad,** a person's present supply of dollar bills or paper money. **Roll** him is to rob him of his money.

Roomer, a lodger who has living accommodation in a house and gets his food elsewhere. (See **Boarder** and **Lodger**).

Roorback, a false story spread about for purposes of political intrigue. The word had its origin in the United States from a flagrant story once issued as an extract from the Travels of Baron **Roorbach.**

Root, to shout, to cheer, to applaud, especially in sport.

Rooter, one who heartily applauds his own side or his favourite players, when a match or game is in progress.

Roper, generally a cowboy, but particularly an expert with the lariat or lasso. (See **Lariat**).

Rotary, a variety of snow-plough placed in front of a railway engine for the purpose of clearing the track.

Rot-gut, drink, of the particularly putrid variety. (See **Drink**).

Rotunda, the hall or main entrance and waiting-room of a railway depot or an hotel.

Rough carpenter. (See **Carpenter**).

Rough-house, a riotous or disorderly house. The scene that would occur in such a place would also be described as **rough-house;** as, "Casey threw a brick, and there was rough-house in quick time." Again it is used to describe the scene on the lacrosse field when players "mix it up" (get too rough).

Round-up, to gather in, to herd in. The round-up is a great event of the year on a big cattle ranch, for then it is that the rancher can brand the foals and calves, and take stock of his belongings. The expression is also used in reference to the beating-up of electors to the poll or of people to a place of meeting.

Roup, a sale by public auction; a word of Scottish origin that is in frequent use in the West.

Route, a word used in a similar sense to the word **delivery** in the Old-Country when applied to the streets covered by a postman, a newspaper boy, or a milkman. A **route boy** brings your morning or evening newspaper, and **route men** or those who make the regular deliveries of milk.

R. S., Revised Statutes of Canada; **R. S. M.,** Revised Statutes of Manitoba.

Rubberneck, the name given by females to men who turn their heads round to ogle them as they pass on the street. Persons who stretch their necks to inquire into other people's affairs are also described as **rubbernecks. Rubber** is also used as a verb. "The men are out to **rubber** at a higher mark than you be," as the mistress remarked to the hired girl who was decking herself out for the stampede.

Rubbers, shoes worn over the ordinary boots, what are known as goloshes in the Old-Country. (See **Overshoes**).

Rube, a farmer or an unsophisticated person in from the country who may be expected to be an easy mark for the city tough or thug. In the Old-Country a **rube** would probably be described as a **joskin.**

Runners, the strips of steel attached to a woodwork frame which take the place of the wheels on a vehicle in winter and thus convert the vehicle into a sleigh.

Runways, the trodden forest paths of deer or other animals, in the direction of water or the feeding grounds.

Rush orders, orders to be completed with the utmost despatch, and to take precedence of all ordinary orders coming into a warehouse or factory. Some customers, however, are so accustomed to mark their orders as **rush orders** that traders sometimes fail to be impressed by the demand for haste. **R.L.H.,** the initials of a profane expression which means an awful rush.

Rust, a blight that comes on certain growing crops during the ripening period. Its chief cause is excessively wet weather or fog.

Rustle, steal; but generally used in connection with cattle-stealing. So' **a rustler** is the name for a cattle thief.

Rye, the commonest and most vitriolic of Canadian and American whiskeys.

S

Sag, to yield, to sink down, to incline from an upright or a horizontal position or from the proper position.

Sakes, a mild exclamation, like **shucks** and others.

Salesman, a commercial traveller, a drummer, a store counter-man, or a man who canvasses real estate.

Sam. To stand Sam is to pay for refreshment or drink, or indeed anything. The term originated in the letters U.S. on the knapsacks of the U.S. soldiers, and which were jocularly said to be the initials of Uncle Sam (the Government), the big paymaster.

Sarcees, an Indian tribe.

Saskatchewan, the great wheat Province situated between Manitoba on the east and Alberta on the west. The Province takes its name from the River Saskatchewan, which in two great branches flows through the Province, and which in the Indian tongue means **swift river.**

Saskatoon, a small wild berry, somewhat resembling the chokecherry, much in favour among the Indians, and from which the prosperous city of Saskatoon takes its name.

Sawbones, a surgeon.

Saw-gang, the gang of men in the lumber camp who do the actual work of tree-felling; the men who ply the axes and saws.

Saw-horse, any simple wooden arrangement whereon to place wood to be sawn. A chopping block, a decrepit saw-horse, an axe, and a rusty buck-saw are the adjuncts of the wood-pile of most Canadian homesteads.

Scab, a blackleg, a man who takes the place of a trade union worker out on strike or locked out

Scads, dollars, money.

Scalawag, a disreputable character, supposed to be capable of any low-down trick.

Scaler, a man in a logging camp who measures the diameter of the logs in each skidway, and so computes the number of board feet in hand.

Scalp (n.), the skin of the top of the head. **Scalp** (v.), to cut off the scalp. In their warlike days, the Indians were accustomed to scalp their fallen enemies, and carry off their scalps as trophies. To be scalped, however, did not mean that an enemy was deprived of his entire hirsute outfit: the noble Indian would turn his victim over on his face, place his knee in the small of the man's back, and, grasping the forelock, would cut away just as much of the scalp as one slash of the knife could accomplish.

Scared, alarmed, frightened, upset. A word used on the smallest pretext.

Schedule (sometimes pronounced **Skedule**), a time-table of trains, sports, business proceedings, etc.

Schooner, a big beer, a long drink, a measure similar to that used in Scottish houses licensed within the meaning of the Act. A remittance man, in reply to the anxious inquiries of his friends, wrote home that he was now engaged in unloading schooners, and the pater wrote back expressing his joy at hearing that his offspring had at last turned his attention to serious work, however laborious. An extra remittance accompanied the pater's letter, and the scion of a noble house proceeded to unload more schooners.

Scoot, to clear out with all the speed you can; and, if a gentleman with a revolver or a brickbat exhorts you to **scoot,** you have to put on some more speed.

Scored, adversely criticised, condemned. When a certain Act of Parliament was severely criticised, an Opposition newspaper came out with the heading "Government Legislation Scored."

Scout, a word sometimes used in saluting a friend, old or young; as, "Hello, old scout."

Scow, a flat-bottomed boat used in the lumber trade; in some places, also, a slow-going old ferry boat.

Scrap, a fight of the promiscuous or impromptu kind. **Scrapper,** a person with a proclivity for making trouble or using his fists

Screen doors, screen windows, additional house fixtures put in during the heat of summer, to permit of ordinary doors and windows being left open and to keep out the mosquitoes, or skeeters.

Scrub, the wild undergrowth of the prairie or unbroken land. (See **Broken**).

Scuffler, a one-horse implement used for cutting the weeds between rows of trees or vegetables.

Sea-level. The height above sea level of Winnipeg is 760 feet, of Montreal 187 feet, of Toronto 350 feet, of Ottawa 294 feet, of Regina 1,885 feet, of Saskatoon 1,571 feet, of Edmonton 2,158 feet, of Calgary 3,389 feet, of Vancouver 136 feet, and of Victoria 85 feet.

Search me (with the emphasis on the second word), I don't know, I can't say. Literally, search me all over for the information you require. **You**

have me there or **You have me beat** are variations of the expression.

Section, 640 acres of land. Each section is divided into four quarter sections, containing 160 acres each. (See **Land**.)

Sectionman, a man in charge of a section of the railway track, who keeps his allotted section in a proper state of repair and guards against accident. He is known as a platelayer in the Old-Country.

Seep, to drip, or drop, or soak in. A contractor put an extra layer of cement round a building to prevent the water **seeping** into the foundation.

Semi-ready, a term used in the tailoring trade, and applied to garments manufactured in some factory in Eastern Canada up to the trying-on stage, after which they are sent West and completed to the correct measurement of the semi-ready tailors' customers.

Senate, the Upper Chamber of the Dominion Parliament, with functions somewhat similar to the British House of Lords. The Lower Chamber is known as the House of Commons.

Set them up, set up the drinks, pay for the round.

Settlement, a word much in vogue in the early days to indicate a district with a considerable population, or the particular portion of that district which was shaping into a village or town. Thus the **Red River Settlement** was the early name of the district of which the city of Winnipeg is now the centre, and the Province of Manitoba grew out of the Red River Settlement.

Settler, an immigrant who permanently makes his home in Canada. **Settlers' effects** include a host of things which the immigrant is allowed to convey into the Dominion duty free and at a cheap rate of transportation.

Shack, a wooden hut, the first modest little dwelling of the homesteader, an erection usually of only one apartment.

Shake, to shake-off, to give a person or an animal "the slip." A traveller moved along to another car to **shake** a bunch of gamblers who had designs on his wad; a lodger moved elsewhere to **shake** undesirable associates; and a man made his way through a crowd to **shake** a dog that persisted in trailing him.

Shake on it, pal! words that, with the shake of the hand, roughly ratify a Western agreement or pledge of friendship.

Shanghai, to drug a seaman and get him on board a ship that is about to sail and is short of hands.

Shanty, a rough, temporary habitation, a degree less pretentious than a shack. (See **Shack**).

Shavings, a carpenter or rough carpenter. (See **Carpenter**).

Sheaf, a bundle of new-cut corn bound together. (See **Shock**).

Shebang, a hut, shanty, shack.

Sheepskin, much used in the make-up of lumberjacks' and other outside workers' winter jackets.

Shenanigan, frolicking, playing tricks, or playing practical jokes. Apparently used either as a noun or a verb.

Shilling. The facetious Canadian will sometimes call the quarter-dollar piece a **shilling**.

Shine, or **Shoe-shine,** having one's boots polished. The words are also used to denote the person who does the work, and the room or shop in which a person gets a **shoe-shine** is also called a **shoe-shine**. A very bald-headed man went into a barber shop and, plumping himself down in the chair, said, "Hair cut!" The barber looked at him for a moment and then replied, "Why, man, you don't need a hair-cut; what you want is a shine."

Shin-plaster, a 25-cent or quarter-dollar note, a curiosity not often seen nowadays.

Shingles, thin wooden boards which take the place of slates for roofing purposes in Canada. Thus, pedestrians in Western cities, in the height of a gale, run no risk of being scalped by a falling slate.

Ship, to pack up and despatch merchandise to a customer who has ordered the goods to be **shipped**.

Shiplap, a quality of lumber commonly used in house-building.

Shipping. When goods are sent or despatched out of town, either by rail or boat, they are said to be **shipped**, and the department of a warehouse which packs them up and despatches them is described as the **shipping** department.

Shirt-waist, a woman's blouse, usually made of different material from the skirt worn with it.

Shirt-waist dance, a dance in which the women taking part are simply dressed, usually in white shirtwaist and dark skirt.

Shirt-waist suit, a woman's one-piece dress; that is, a dress in which bodice and skirt are joined.

Shivaree (properly **Charivari**), a mock serenade of discordant music; usually a tremendous banging of tin cans, a fitful popping of six-shooters, and an abortive attempt at a procession. If the "boys" succeed in keeping moderately sober, however, the **shivaree** may be a great success.

Shock, a pile of sheaves of wheat or other crops. (See **Sheaf**).

Shoepacks, moccasins made from cowhide, either oil-tanned or otherwise, and with which a person may wear felt insoles or an extra pair of socks. (See **Moccasins**).

Shoes. This term in Canada includes both the walking shoes and the laced boots of the Old-Country, though a distinction is made by calling one lot **low shoes** and the other **high shoes.** The word **boots** is only applied to boots that come up over the calf of the leg and are generally pulled on without lacing.

Shooting-iron, a revoler, a gun.

Shooting off, telling a tale or interjecting remarks *t*hat are out of place or that nobody is anxious to hear. **Shooting off hot air is a** common expression and might be interpreted as talking for talking's sake.

Shooting the rapids, navigating the fast-flowing portion of a river, a feat of daring in which Indians excel, but which sometimes ends in disaster. (See **Portage**).

Shoot up the town, might be interpreted as meaning to run amuck, or to go on the rampage with a revolver. In the old lawless days, in certain Western communities, when a man went **shooting up the town,** he was usually mad drunk, and, though he fired indiscriminately and sent the population indoors to seek shelter under the bed, the providence which protects drunken men and bairns generally prevented him from being guilty of murder. After his escapade, the shooter would likely return to the saloon and set up the drinks. "When he was a little shaver his parents were quite strict; He never played with other boys—ma feared he would get licked; Pa never took him to a show; he'd never seen a park; In fact, the youngster never knew a joyous boyhood lark. They told him he'd an angel be, and they'd supply the wings, But as the pet grew older he cut loose the heavenly strings. His early training was a frost; he did not win renown, He's boarding in Stillwater now for 'shooting up' a town."

Shot, a drink of liquor, a horn, a snort; one of the many forms of invitation to imbibe is, "Come on, old sport, and have a **shot.**" A man who is **shot** is a man who is drunk.

Shot-gun, the larger weapon, used for sport or killing game. (See **Gun**).

Shower, a word used in reference to several interesting social events similar to the "surprise party" in the Old-Country. For instance, a lady on the eve of her wedding may be given a **linen shower,** on which occasion her friends will assemble and shower upon her various gifts of linen to start housekeeping; or it may be a **tin shower,** when her practically-minded well-wishers will derive much amusement by trying to besiege her with a supply of kitchen and other household utensils; and so on, ad lib. **Showers** generally precede a wedding.

Shucks, a common and innocent exclamation which may mean anything from "dearie me!" to "Holy Moses!"

Shuswaps, a tribe of Indians, with their habitat in British Columbia.

Shy, short, scarce. **Shy on funds,** short of cash, hard up. **A few months shy of twenty,** a few months short of twenty years of age.

Side line, an additional department of a business or of a traveller's trade. A traveller who takes an occasional order for a firm other than his regular employers does it **on the side.**

Side order, a dish which is not on the day's menu at a restaurant, but which may be specially ordered and specially cooked.

Sidestepping, wandering from the argument, evading the question.

Sidetracked, knocked out of the running, defeated by adverse circumstances or powerful opposition, pushed on to the scrap-heap.

Sidewalk, that part of both sides of the street reserved for foot passengers, that part known as the pavement in the Old-Country.

Silo, a tall, circular, air-tight building or structure for preserving green fodder.

Silver State, Nevada, which is also known as the **Sage-hen State.**

Simoleon, a dollar. (See **Dollar** for other names).

Siwash, a tribe of Indians.

Siwash, a mean, contemptible, worthless person; a term of address that is intended to give offence, as **"You Siwash!"**

Six-shooter, a six-chambered revolver, though a revolver of any number of chambers may be so described at times.

Skate, an old horse. A person who is lapsing into a state of dotage is sometimes referred to as an **old skate.**

Skating, one of the most popular of Canadian winter pastimes on the rivers and in the rinks. Great speed and skill is acquired, and a fancy skater will cut with his skates on the ice the outline of animals, buildings, flowers, etc.

Skedaddle, to make a hasty departure, to bolt, to scamper off, to scoot.

Skeered, scared, frightened.

Skeeter, a mosquito. (See **Mosquito**).

Skid, to slide a lumber log down an incline to the skidway, where the logs are temporarily stacked until the big drive.

Skiddoo, get off, get out, make tracks.

Skinned, licked, beaten; as, "Our little burg is going ahead; it has all other places **skinned**"; or, "Asquith is an excellent debater, though for purity of style and elegance of diction Sir Wilfrid or Borden have him **skinned** forty ways."

Skinner, a teamster in a lumber camp, so called because he is supposed to drive a pair of "old skins" or "skates."

Sky pilot, a parson, one who points life's mariners to mansions in the skies.

Skyscraper, a very lofty building. **Skyscraper man,** the name given to the workman who performs the perilous work of erecting the steel framework of the skyscraper.

Sled (or **sleigh**), the Canadian boy's chief outdoor plaything in winter, taking the place of the summer go-cart, and with it he does his chores and runs errands. Some boys are in happy possession of a dog which he can yoke to the sled, and the turn-out forms a pretty picture that amuses newcomers.

Sleever, a long drink, a big glass of beer, much like a schooner. (See **Schooner**).

Sleigh, a vehicle mounted on runners, for the conveyance of individuals or merchandise. All sorts are to be seen in Canada in the dead of winter, from the handsome, picturesque, private family outfit to the heavy, lumbering freight-sleigh of the contractor or the railway companies. A low sleigh is known as a **cutter,** and a high sleigh is a **speeder.**

Slewed, drunk, or intoxicated. Originally a seaman's word, derived from the way in which a ship sometimes tacks, gliding off at another angle. The course generally pursued by a drunken, or **slewed,** man is something like that of a ship.

Slick, quick, expert, clever, smart.

Slim, tricky.

Slogan, a war-cry, an election cry; a word which had its origin in the Highlands of Scotland, but is now in frequent use in Canada, especially at election times.

Slouch, a lazy and lazy-looking person.

Slough (pronounced **slew**), a hollow in the prairie that fills up during the wet season, and from which, when the dry season comes, some excellent hay is obtained. (See **Muskeg**).

Smock, a working jacket, supposed to correspond with the overalls. (See **Overalls**).

Smoke. (See **Watch my smoke**).

Smooth, polite and oily. **Smooth trick,** a swindle so neatly performed that you thought the person was doing you a service. **Smooth guy,** the "nice, pleasant, affable person" who soaks you in the most bare-faced manner.

Smudge, an out-door smoldering fire made so that it will produce much smoke to drive mosquitoes away.

Snag, any unsuspected obstacle in a river or elsewhere.

Snake-room, a side room or a basement where saloon-keepers accommodate doped or drunken people until they recover their senses; presumably a place where they "see snakes."

Snakes, delirium tremens.

Snap, a cinch, something worth securing or easily secured. Real estate agents are fond of describing their "good things" as snaps.

Snap-apple night, Hallowe'en.

Snort, a drink. The sporting Canadian asks his friend, "Will you have a snort?"

Snorting around, nosing around, or (in the case of a person in authority) wandering around in a snarling, fault-finding humour.

Snow, frozen or crystallized vapor.

Snow. When the snow flies is that period of the year when snow first makes its appearance, and when the flakes are so light and filmy that they float or fly a long time in the air before alighting to earth. Thus, when the poet or novelist uses the phrase he refers to the coming of winter.

Snow-blindness, temporary blindness caused by the glare of sunlight reflected from the snow, and sometimes caused merely by gazing too long on the clean white snow, without relieving the eyes by changing the object of vision for something dark.

Snow-bound, snowed-up, or imprisoned by snow, no uncommon experience in Canada either at home or when travelling on the railway.

Snow-broth, snow and water mixed; hence very cold liquor.

Snow-bunting, a finch of the Arctic regions which comes south during the winter; a snowbird.

Snow-cock, a snow-partridge.

Snowdrift, a bank of snow drifted or piled up by the wind.

Snow-eater, a Chinook or warm wind which rapidly melts the snow.

Snow fence, an embankment of snow raised on the windward side of a railway or other road as some protection against a snowstorm.

Snow-flea, a leaping insect, found on the snow in such numbers as to become a pest in some parts.

Snow-line, the line on a mountain slope above which there is snow all the year round.

Snow-plow, a plough-like arrangement on a large scale for clearing away the snow from roads, railways, etc.

Snow-shoes, a shoe, or racket-shaped arrangement, worn to prevent the feet from sinking into the snow. Snowshoeing is a popular sport, and many people acquire great speed in walking or running with the curious footgear.

Soak, to rob, swindle, or drive a dishonest bargain. The person who is soaked is called a **sucker.**

Soft drinks, a general term which includes lemonade, ginger beer, and all non-intoxicating beverages.

Solicitor, a canvasser for goods or publications.

Sombrero, a broad-brimmed hat of Spanish or Mexican shape.

Some is used in many ways that strike the new-comer as distinctly amusing. **That's some congregation** will refer to a church that is packed to the doors; **That's some hat** will refer to the enormous creation with which a lady's head is adorned; **That's some horse,** referring to a particularly fine animal; **That's going some** may mean great speed or excellence of workmanship, or it may even be used in reference to the speed at which a person races to his ruin; **That's some cigar is a cigar** to be admired; and the simple words **And then some** are often added as an afterthought, to suggest that there is any amount of excellence expected or held in reserve. **"Some walkers these"** was the inscription under a photographic group of pedestrians; and a facetious editor put the heading **"Some Wedding"** above the following paragraph: "The groom is a successful physician of this city, a young gentleman of splendid work, and brilliant promise, for he is endowed by birth and training with all those noble impulses and winsome traits that adorn true manhood. The bride is a lady of wondrous fascination and remarkable attractiveness, for, with manners as enchanting as the wand of a siren and a disposition as sweet as the odors of flowers, and spirits as joyous as the caroling of birds, and mind as brilliant as those glittering tresses that adorn the brow of winter, and with heart as pure as dewdrops trembling in a coronet of violets, she will make the home of her husband a paradise of enchantment like the lovely home of her girlhood, where the heaven-toned harp of marriage, with its chords of love and devotion and fond endearments sent forth the sweetest strains of felicity that ever thrilled the senses with the rhythmic pulsings of ecstatic rapture."

Some. A further illustration of the use of the word: "When it's colder than the dickens, And **some more** on top of that; When the chill tube gets the ague And marks minus-thirty flat; When the frosty perspiration On your alabaster brow Takes the form of frigid dewdrops, It's **some** chilly, you'll allow."

Songhees, a tribe of Indians. The site of the city of Victoria, on Vancouver Island, was once a portion of their hunting ground.

Sons of England, a benefit society, applicants for membership of which are supposed to be of English birth or parentage.

Sore, annoyed, riled, nasty, vexed. Don't get **sore,** don't get nasty, don't lose your temper. Was **sore** about it, felt annoyed over the matter.

Sore-head, a person who sees trouble and wickedness in everything.

Sorrel, a dock-like plant of a reddish-brown colour. **Sorrel** is thus spoken of as a colour, and usually referring to the colour of a horse.

Soused, loaded up with drink.

Space, or Space work, the accepted contributions of promiscuous reporters or men not actually on the staff or pay-roll; similar to the penny-a-liner work, or lineage, in the Old-Country.

Spank, to punish, whip, chastise a child; usually over the parents' knee and on the spot ordained by nature. **Spanking,** chastisement.

Sow-belly, bacon.

Sparrow, an immigrant from London, England

Speeder. (See **Sleigh**).

Speeding, the common offence of motorists or cyclists known as **scorching** in the Old-Country.

Spellbinder, a humorous designation for a political or public speaker, who "binds as by a spell." Any platform speaker may, however, be seriously or sarcastically described as a **spellbinder.**

'Spiel, contraction for **Bonspiel,** a curling tournament.

Spiel, spout, preach, lecture, a derisive term used in reference to a wordy admonition.

Split-log, a device used for levelling roads.

Spoils system, the granting of office or employment for political reasons rather than efficiency.

Spondulics, money, the ready, the wherewithal to pay.

Sport, one who will take his chances in life or death, in a small gamble or a big gamble; and the genuine **sport** will take no advantage which is not equally within reach of his opponent.

Sport. Hello, old sport! a common form of salutation among men; but should not be used in church circles and not often at the rooms of the Y.M.C.A.

Spot. Dollar bills or notes are sometimes spoken of as a one-spot, two-spot, and so on. This word, however, is most frequently applied in reference to the five-dollar bill, which is a **five-spot.**

Spotted dog, plum pudding.

Spread-eagle, or Spread-eagleism, the patriotic brag of an American.

Spruce, trim, tidy, lively. **Spruce up,** buck up, liven yourself, get dressed.

Sprung, intoxicated; sometimes, also, the word is used in reference to a person who is alleged to be eccentric or off his balance.

Spur track, a railway siding or a short branch line which runs into factory or warehouse premises.

Square deal, term often used in reference to a straight transaction. When men go out on strike in Canada their cry is that they want a **square deal;** or in any dispute both parties will protest that they are open for a **square deal.** A straightforward and avowedly honest transaction is said to be **on the square;** and a **raw deal** is an unfair or dishonest deal.

Square meal, an abundant meal, enough to satisfy the appetite.

Squat, to take up a homestead or settle down on some new land.

Squaw, an Indian wife or woman.

Squaw-man, a white man who is married to an Indian woman.

Squaw tale, an old woman's story, a prophecy of evil, a very unintelligent anticipation of events that will never occur.

Squeal, to bemoan a loss or misfortune. "'Tis music in the gambler's ear to hear the sucker squeal." To **squeal** also means to confess, or divulge a secret, or "let up" on confederates in mischief. Thus, the person who turns king's evidence is said to have **squealed.**

Stack, generally a large pile of hay, grain or straw, though it may be applied to anything from a handful of coin upwards.

Stack, a pile of lumber; a rollway of logs decked on the banks of the river ready for the drive.

Stag party, a gathering of men only. A party consisting entirely of women is called a **tabby party.**

Stake, a debt, a score, the bill which the lumberjack runs up at the saloon or the general store.

Stake, the little pile of earnings which is due to the harvester, the lumberjack and others at the end of the season's work. (See also **Grubstake).**

Stakes, posts by which holdings or claims are marked out.

Stampede, properly a wild flight of maddened or frightened horses or cattle, but the word has also been adopted as a picturesque name for shows and exhibitions of the Wild West description.

Stand for, agree to, or put up with. Thus in Canada a person will say **I won't stand for it** in a case in which, in the Old-Country, one would say **I won't stand it.**

Stars and Stripes, the United States Flag, the Star-spangled Banner, the Gridiron. **Stars and Bars,** the Confederate Flag during the Civil War, 1861-65.

Stay with the job, see the thing through.

Steep story, a stretch of the imagination. (See **Tall story.)**

Steerer. (See **Bunco-steerer).**

Stetson, a soft felt hat of the cowboy style of headgear.

Stewed, one of the many words used to describe the condition of a drunken man.

Stick around, wait about, hang around, or loaf around. The Canadian sport will **stick around** in the expectation of meeting the boys and having a good time.

Sticker, a person who holds on to his work or post. (See **Quitter).**

Stiff, a corpse, or about as valueless as a corpse. Frequently used in reference to players who are of no use in the game.

Stock, in the printing and stationery trade the paper used for a job is known as the **stock,** and the word also applies to the paper used in the production of a book. The cheaper qualities of paper used for newspapers is known as **newsprint.**

Stockmen, generally understood to be the men who trade in cattle, purchasing on the farms and ranches and forwarding the stock to the stockyards, but ranchers and their managers are also included in the term.

Stockyards, the railway sidings or enclosures where import and export of cattle is conducted.

Stogie, a bad, cheap cigar; one of splendid appearance, but of the cabbage brand.

Stomach-robber, the cook in a lumber or construction camp; sometimes also called **dough-slinger.**

Stoney, generally describes the position of a man who has spent his last dollar, or is **stoney broke;** but it is also the name of a tribe of Indians.

Stook, a bunch of sheaves (eight or ten) of grain placed in an upright position on the harvest field for drying purposes before being carted to the thresher.

Stoop, the porch at the front or side of the house; a landing with steps leading down to the street or garden.

Stop-off or **Stop-over privileges,** an arrangement made with the ticket agent to break a railway journey at some place where the passenger wishes to make a short halt.

Store, a shop, any retail establishment.

Stork. On the occasion of a birth, the **Stork** is said to have flown over or visited the happy home. Thus when a new baby is about to arrive, it is said that a visit from the **Stork** is expected.

Stove, a portable fireplace, of which there are many different varieties and sizes.

Stovepipe, the pipe leading from the stove to the chimney, usually giving out its warmth to the upper chambers on its way.

Stovepipe hat, an old-fashioned high hat.

Straight, a phrase peculiar to drinkers, and similar to the English word neat, unmixed with water.

Strathconas, the general name for officers and men of Lord Strathcona's

Horse (Royal Canadians), a popular corps of the Canadian permanent force. The regiment was first formed for service in the South African war.

Streamers, the Aurora Borealis, Northern Lights.

Street railway, tram-lines. **Street car,** the cars run on the street railway. The same are known in the Old-Country as tramcars.

Strike, reach, or arrive. "I hope to **strike** Vancouver within five days after leaving Montreal."

Stubble, that part of the grain stalk below where it is cut to be bound into sheaves.

Stuck, stung. (See **Stung**).

Stuck upon himself, full of self-conceit and confidence.

Stuff, money, or means.

Stumpage, standing trees, as viewed by the lumberman in his trade calculations; the amount of standing timber available for cutting.

Stung, bitten, sold, taken in. **Severely stung,** got what he didn't bargain for; though, perhaps, the real old-timer would use the phrase, **stung good and hard.**

Stunt, something done. 'A good stunt, something smart. A new stunt, a new idea.

Sub-basement, the lower flat of a building which has two flats below the level of the street. The flat immediately below the level of the street is the **basement.** (See **Basement**).

Subdivision. Each section of surveyed Canadian land (i.e., 640 acres) is deemed to be divided into sixteen 40-acre areas, which are known as legal subdivisions; and these subdivisions are again divided into lots, which are exploited by the proprietors or real estate agents as building lots.

Sucker, a person easily imposed on, one who snaps at any bait, a victim of crooks and dishonest people, a regular loser at cards or other games of chance, one who readily absorbs the con. man's guff.

Sucker State, Illinois; and the people of Illinois are nicknamed **Suckers.** A well-known Illinois politician was speaking at the same banquet with a governor of New Jersey. The Jersey governor went into exhaustive figures as to the wealth and agricultural and manufacturing resources of his own State, and, before he sat down, he said: "I am to be followed by a silver-tongued orator from Illinois, and I hope before he sits down he will tell us why they are called 'suckers.' " Our friend from Illinois said: "Mr. Toastmaster, when I heard the speech of the gentleman from New Jersey I was almost ashamed to come from the corn belt of Illinois, and when he told us of his State's manufactures it made Illinois look small, but I noticed Mr. Toastmaster, that you and the gentlemen

about you seemed incredulous—in fact, I could tell by your expression that you did not believe a word he said. Now, I want to say to the Governor of New Jersey that I believe every word he said, and that is the reason I am called a sucker."

Suicide, a word that is used both as a noun and as a verb. "Horse thief suicides by drowning" was the heading of a paragraph which told of the act of suicide.

Sulky, a one-horse, two-wheeled vehicle, with a seat for one person only. Used now only in trotting matches.

Summer. (See **Indian summer**).

Summer fallowing, preparing the fallow land. (See **Fallow**).

Sundae, a summer delicacy consisting of ice-cream and a topping of strawberries, raspberries, or some flavoured sweetmeat.

Sun-dog, a parhelion, mock sun, appearing in the form of a bright light near the sun, and sometimes having colours like the rainbow. Sometimes there are several, appearing at the same height above the horizon as the true sun. Their cause is certain modifications which light undergoes when it falls on the crystals of ice or minute particles that constitute clouds.

Sundowner, a tramp, an overlander, an overland-mailer; a man who blows in to some Western camp about sunset, asking for work, which he knows cannot be obtained at that hour, but who is usually accommodated with rest and refreshment. Sometimes called a **Whaler,** from his habit of cruising about the country.

Sun in the eyes, too much drink. A person who is under the influence of drink is said to have the **sun in his eyes** or to have been **standing too long in the sun.**

Sun-up, sunrise.

Sure, a common expression, meaning "Of course" or "Certainly," and used much the same as it is used in Ireland, though Canadians will resent the suggestion that the expression is of Irish origin. **Sure thing** means "That's a certainty."

Swamp, low-lying, soft, wet ground, a fresh-water bog.

Swamper, the man who cuts and clears the roots from the narrow trails through the forest from the standing timber to the skidway at the edge of the logging road; he also cuts the limbs off the felled trees.

Swat, to hit, strike, smite; and the **swatting** may be directed at either a person or a party. In a country paper recently it was stated that the local Conservatives were "preparing to take another **swat** at the Liberals, and they were going to **swat the Liberals good and hard.**"

Sweater, a worsted winter jacket, with fancy buttons and braiding of a bright colour; a characteristic Canadian winter garment.

Swipe, steal. One of the many slang expressions imported from the Old-Country, and Canadianised.

Switch, the lever at a junction of railway lines by which a train is **switched** on to another line. **Points** they are called in the Old-Country.

Switchman, or **Switch-tender,** a railway pointsman. **Asleep at the switch,** a metaphor to suggest unwatchfulness or asleep on duty.

T

Tab, keep tab on him, keep a watch on him, or dog his footsteps.

Tabby party, a gathering of women only. A party consisting entirely of men is termed a **stag party.**

Talkee-talkee, jargon, a corrupt dialect.

Tall. A tall **story,** one that is more imaginative than truthful.

Tang, a distinct and characteristic taste or flavour, or a taste of something extraneous to the thing itself; as, **the wine had a tang of the cork,** or **there was a tang of malice in his speech.**

Tanglefoot, whiskey. (See **Drink**).

Tank, a jag. **A tank on,** filled up with drink. (See **Jag**).

Teach school is how a Canadian school teacher describes his duties. A glance over the Canadian "Who's Who" shows that an enormous number of the enlightened men of the Dominion have **taught school** at some period of their lives.

Team, a pair of horses, mules, or oxen; and the term generally includes the wagon to which the animals are attached. The man in charge of the outfit if asked his occupation will reply that he **drives a team.**

Teepee, Indian word for **tent.** Canadians who have had much intercourse with Indians will sometimes use the word in referring to their houses or places of dwelling.

Teeter, or **Teeter-totter,** the see-saw swing of the children's playground.

Teetotal. About the beginning of last century a temperance society at Hector, New York, pledged themselves to abstain from distilled spirits only, but ten years later another pledge bound all signers to total abstinence, the two classes being distinguished by the initials O. P. (old pledge) and T. (total). T total thus became a familiar term, and it gradually took the word form of teetotal.

Telescope, a box-shaped hold-all or grip of basket-work or leather consisting of two parts, the lid or outer section being slightly larger than the inner section, and fitting over it. A couple of straps and a strap handle complete the arrangement for carrying as luggage.

Tenderfoot, a word used in the wilder Far West to indicate a new-comer or greenie who does not readily adapt himself to Western manners and customs. Usually he is the butt and mark of the toughs and frolicsome old-timers.

Ten-forty, a five per cent. bond issued by the United States Government in 1864, during the Civil War, redeemable at any time after ten years and payable in forty years.

Texas, originally the upper deck of a Mississippi steamboat, but now the word has reached the Pacific and is used to indicate the upper deck of the coasting steamers.

Texas-tender, a waiter serving on the Texas, or upper deck.

That's too bad! another exclamation of sympathy, of the feminine kind.

There, all complete, smart. **All there,** smart, has all his wits, nothing wanting. **Get there,** to achieve on object. Also to **Get there with both feet.** (See **Feet**).

There's a reason, a common remark and frequently the footnote to an advertisement. A notorious bum is known to be hanging round one of the boys, and **there's a reason,** viz., that the bum is on the borrow. The Empress Theatre is packed every night, and **there's a reason,** the excellence of the programme, of course. Stedman's boots are in great demand, and **there's a reason,** the reason being the high quality of the goods.

Thimble party, a social gathering of women intent on getting through a lot of needlework, which may be for a personal or a charitable purpose.

Three for a nickel! Long the cry of the Winnipeg newsies, the evening editions of the three papers ("Free Press," "Telegram," and "Tribune") being sold at the price of a nickel for the three.

Through, done, finished. The word is used in the same sense as it is in some parts of Scotland. **I am through** with it, I've finished the job.

Thrown down, an intensification of the **turned down** treatment, to be **thrown down** being to be deliberately slighted, insulted or injured. The Parliamentary candidate who was defeated by a few votes was merely **turned down;** whereas the person rejected by an overwhelming majority was **thrown down.**

Thug, a murderous thief.

Ticket, the printed list of candidates in an election, the policy, the platform. **Straight ticket,** the party nominations. **Split ticket,** a divided policy, a ticket bearing names of candidates representing different interests. **Mixed ticket,** a list of names in which the interests of different parties have been blended.

Tickle-brain, strong drink.

Ties. What are known as railway sleepers in the Old-Country are called **ties** in Canada. No "chairs" are used, the rails being spiked direct to the ties.

Tie-up, a blockade, an obstruction, a stoppage of work or progress.

Tightwad, a miser, a stingy person.

Timber-r-r! the long-drawn melodious warning call of the sawyers in a lumber camp when a tree is about to fall.

Timber, generally understood to mean standing trees, large enough to cut into **logs,** and when the logs are cut up into boards, planks, joists, etc., they are known as **lumber.** The cutting and hauling of this timber is known in some districts as **lumbering** and in others as **logging.**

Timber limits, the lots or holdings of each contractor, or the limits set by Government.

Timber permit. A homesteader, on application and the payment of a nominal fee, can obtain a permit to cut for his own use a stated number of lineal feet of timber on Government lands.

Time (Difference of). The difference between Canadian time and Greenwich or London time is as follows: Halifax, Nova Scotia, 4 hours 14 minutes; Montreal, 4 hrs. 54 mins.; Toronto, 5 hrs.; Winnipeg, 6 hrs. 28 mins.; Vancouver, B.C., 8 hrs. 12 mins. Thus, when it is midday in London it is 8.46 a.m. in Halifax, 7.6 a.m. at Montreal, 7 a.m. at Toronto, 5.32 a.m. at Winnipeg, and 3.48 a.m. at Vancouver.

Time in Canada. There are five divisions of Standard Time in Canada. Atlantic time is four hours behind Greenwich time, and Eastern, Central, Mountain and Pacific time have a difference of one hour between each. On the Canadian Pacific Railway it is Atlantic time east of Vanceboro; Eastern time from Vanceboro to Fort William and Sault Ste. Marie; Central time west of Sault Ste. Marie and Fort William to Broadview; Mountain time from Broadview to Laggan; Pacific time from Laggan to Vancouver. Municipalities have generally adopted Standard time.

Time of my life, another expressive phrase used when a person is telling of having had a good time.

Timothy, an authority describes it as "a very poor pasture grass, but undoubtedly the most popular hay plant we have."

Tinclad, a musket-proof gunboat such as were used on the American rivers during the Civil War, the armour-plating of these being very light. Nowadays, however, the word **tin-clad** is in common use in the Western building trade as an adjective in reference to frame houses, vehicles, doors, or household fittings that have been encased in a covering of tin

Tired. You make me tired is one of the expressive phrases used by the Canadian to intimate that he has had enough of your presence or your importunity

Toadskin, a dollar bill. Originally, in the States, a **toadskin** meant a five-cent stamp, and of a mean, grasping person it was said "His purse is made of toad's skin."

Toboggan, a long sled, curved back at the front, used in the sport of coasting down-hill. **Toboggan-slide,** the part of the hill on which the **tobogganing** is done.

Tobogganning, a recreation enjoyed by young folks chiefly, during the winter season. One or several persons take a reclining position on a toboggan or long sled at the brow of a steep hill covered with ice. The boy in the rear uses a foot like a rudder to guide the load on its career to the bottom. The propelling power is its own momentum, and the speed is sometimes terrific.

Tom, Dick and Harry, everybody and anybody.

Tomahawk, an Indian's war hatchet, which was used either at close quarters or thrown at an enemy, and with wonderful precision.

Tombs (The), the New York city prison.

Too bad! an exclamation of sympathy. If you tell a Canadian that you are unwell, or that you "feel a bit tough," he is likely to exclaim "That's too bad!" or "Too bad, too bad!"

Toot, a laudatory speech. On a toot, on a spree.

Tooth-carpenter, a dentist.

Toothpick, a very tall and thin person. Also jocularly spoken of as the last of the four courses of a boarding-house dinner, viz., soup, roast, pudding, and toothpick.

Topnotch, or **Topnotcher,** a person at the head of the trade, business, profession, game, or anything else.

Toque, a woman's small hat fitting the head closely. (See **Tuque**).

Tort, a wrong or injury remediable by an action for damages.

Tote, originally meant to haul supplies, particularly food, by road, to a railway construction or lumber camp.

Tote. Tote him round, trot him round to see the sights.

Totee, or **Toter,** the driver of a tote-sleigh.

Tote road, the trail or road over which provisions and supplies are conveyed to a working camp.

Tote-sleigh, a sled on which provisions and supplies are carried to a lumber camp.

Touched, tapped, borrowed, robbed. "He **touched** me for five dollars," he robbed me of five dollars."

Tough, hardened in the ways of the world. **A tough,** a man who is not too scrupulous in his dealings with his fellow-men, or who is on the lookout for victims to fleece or maltreat

Tough. To **feel tough** is to feel unwell or out of sorts, just the opposite of what the expression means in the Old-Country.

Tough yarn, an incredible story, more imaginative than truthful.

Tourist car, the class of railway car between the **Pullman** and the **tourist,** about equalling the second-class accommodation on Old-Country lines. (See **Pullman** and **Colonist**).

Township, a square piece of land containing thirty-six sections of about one square mile each. (See **Land**).

Townsite. The land adjacent to the spot selected by a railway company for a station, and on which it is expected a town will grow up.

Track, the railroad, which in many parts of Western Canada is practically a public highway when there is not a convenient trail or public road. To **make tracks,** to go or run away. **Off the track,** out of one's reckoning, or on the wrong scent.

Trade, an exchange, or a swop. As a preliminary to some exchange of articles, a Westerner may say "I'll do a trade with you," or "I'll trade my clock (watch) for your gun (revolver)."

Trader, used particularly in reference to the men who traded in the old days with the Indians; the men who "dickered and swopped strings of beads for skins of bears."

Trail, the rough, ill-defined roads of the West. The **Long Trail,** a long, cross-country trail. The **Long Trail,** or the **Lone Trail,** is sometimes, also, the journey beyond the grave. **Trail** is also used as a verb, meaning to follow or track a person; or a dog may **trail** his master or **trail** a culprit.

Trailer, a scout, an expert in tracking an enemy, desperadoes, or wild animals.

Train crew, a term borrowed from seafaring life, and meaning all the men who work a railway train.

Trainmen, the train crew, the men who work the railway train.

Transient, a passing visitor, or only an occasional caller or customer. The **transient** is the person who may be treated right royally, or have to pay 50 for a 25-cent meal—all according to the temperament of mine host.

Transportation, carrying by rail or other means. "I've got my transportation" is what a Canadian will say when he has got his railway fare all right, all right.

Trap (verb), to set traps for game or wild animals, though the hunter, going out only with his gun, may say he is going out **trapping**.

Trapper, a hunter, or a man whose occupation it is to entrap wild animals for their fur.

Trash, a negro term of contempt.

Treed, hunters or belated travellers driven up a tree by wolves, bears, or other animals.

Trek, to move off, to seek new land. Of South African origin.

Trim (noun), lumber of the finer grade used for interior and exterior building purposes. The doors, windows, mouldings, interior finish, etc., is usually called **the trim.**

Trouble. (See **Looking for trouble**).

Truck, junk, rubbish. **Truck farm,** where miscellaneous kitchen garden produce is cultivated.

Trusty, a convict with special privileges and considerable freedom, as, for instance, being sent to do road or garden work beyond the penitentiary bounds.

Try-out, a trial, a rehearsal, an experimental effort, a preliminary canter. A young man had just proposed marriage in apparently quite an original little speech, when he was informed by the young lady that he had already proposed to her sister in exactly the same words. "But, darling," declared the ready-witted youth, "that was only a **try-out**: this is the first professional performance."

Tuckered out, dead beat, done up; usually referring to a person's bodily strength.

Tuque (pronounced **tuke**), a woollen cap worn by a child, usually running to a peak, which ends with a tassel, said peak and tassel hanging down by the side of the head when the tuque is in use.

Turkey, a lumberman's working outfit, including bag or sack, clothing, and blankets. Harvesters and railway construction workers occasionally also describe their kit as their **turkey.**

Turned down, refused, not listened to. "The appeal was turned down cold." A person who has been snubbed or an unsuccessful applicant for a position or office is also said to have been **turned down,** and a person to whom you offer, say a cigar, will accept and remark "I never **turn down** a good cigar." Paradoxical as it may seem, the same person may remark, "I never **pass up** a good cigar," which means the same thing as **turn down.**

Turpentine State, North Carolina; the people are known as **Tarheels.**

Twin Cities, when spoken of in Canada, usually refer to Port Arthur and Fort William, neighboring cities and ports in Ontario, situated on Thunder Bay, Lake Superior.

Twirler, a baseball pitcher.

Twist on the shorts, a Wall Street phrase, used when the shorts have undersold heavily, and the market has been artificially raised, causing them to sell at a heavy loss.

U

U.E.L., United Empire Loyalists, British subjects who remained loyal to the Crown when the American Colonies broke away. Many Canadians are now proud of their U. E. L. descent.

Ugly, nasty, spiteful. **Don't get ugly,** don't get nasty, don't get sore. **Ugliness**, ill-nature, perversity.

Unbleached American, a coloured native of the United States, a "gentleman of colour."

Uncork, to lay bare, expose to view; to tell the whole story.

Uncle, a familiar mode of address, varied sometimes by **Dad.**

Uncle Sam. (See **Sam**).

Under, out, dead, submerged in difficulties. (See **Down and out**).

Under dog, the man in trouble, the person who is being defeated, or who is having the worst of it in a dispute or a fight.

Underground railway, an American organisation of the old slavery days which assisted fugitive slaves to the free States and Canada.

Under the weather, may sometimes mean what the words actually imply, suffering from the effect of the weather; but usually it means that the individual is drinking or at home recovering from the effects of drink.

Ungava, the former name of the northern portion of the peninsula of Labrador, between the east shore of Hudson Bay and the Atlantic, but which now forms part of the Province of Quebec.

Unicorn, a team of horses, two wheelers abreast and a leader in front.

Unload, to sell stocks, shares or articles of merchandise that have been held in expectation of a rise in price.

Up-a-daisy, or Ups-a-daisy, the tender words of the fond father when engaged in baby-jumping.

Up against it, in a trying position, facing a difficult problem, at the last extremity. A Canadian is **up against it** when he has a big difficulty to surmount, some unpleasantness to face, or when he has reached the end of his resources.

Upper ten, originally applied to the wealthy classes of New York, but now in general use in all cities.

Uptown, the upper part of a town or city.

Up to you, depends on you, we look to you. "It is up to Mr. Borden to fulfil his election promises," "It is up to the C.P.R. to provide the car service." "It is up to the night watchman to see that no more hoboes frequent the premises," "It is up to the Caledonian Society to provide a fitting welcome for the Scottish curlers," are extracts from a newspaper, which all show how the phrase is used. **"Up to him"** was the heading given by the same journal to the following item: He— "If I should kiss you, what would happen?" She—"I should call father." He—"Then, I won't do it." She—"But father's in Europe."

Use. No use for him is an expression used in reference to an undesirable person, an incompetent workman, or anything under discussion. "I have no use for him, and so have cut him out."

V

V, five dollars or a five-dollar bill.

Vagrant, commonly called a **Vag**, one who has no visible means of subsistence. When a man is arrested as a vag. he must either go to prison or hike out of the town.

Valley tan, a special distillation of whiskey sold in Utah.

Vamoose, or Vamose, to decamp, to clear out quickly. Also **vamoosed** and **vamoosing. Vamoose the ranch**, get off the ranch.

Vancouver, the commercial metropolis of British Columbia and the mainland terminus of the Canadian Pacific Railway. Incorporated in 1886, it is the largest centre of population in British Columbia, has fine streets, and magnificent buildings that vie with the best in older Canadian cities.

Varsity, university; a word first used at Oxford, but now in general use in Canada and the States.

Velocipede, the three-wheeled bogie on which section-men and linemen move up and down the railway in repairing expeditions. The propelling rod attached to the axle is worked by hand in much the same fashion as a pump, and the little vehicle is simply hitched off the line on the approach of a train.

Venireman, citizen summoned to serve as a juror. In the States, many are called, but few are chosen, the contending lawyers in all important trials finding great sport in the challenging process, which appears to be a combined effort to prove that not one in the whole bunch is eligible to serve. The word appears in the Canadian newspapers, but is not in use in the Dominion courts— only in the United States courts.

Venison, the flesh of a deer.

Veterans who have seen active service in defence of Canada and the Empire are enrolled in the Imperial Veterans' Association of Canada.

Veterinarian, a veterinary surgeon, or an inspector of live-stock and stabling.

Victoria, the seat of Government and the capital of British Columbia, is situated on the south-east of Vancouver Island. The Parliament

(49)

Building, overlooking James Bay, is one of the finest examples of architecture in the New World.

Victoria Day, May 24, a Dominion holiday.

Vigilance committee, a body of men self-constituted for the purpose of protecting the public interests and administering justice in districts where the recognised authorities appeared to be powerless to cope with disorders. **Vigilant,** a member of such a committee. (See Lynch).

Village. A Western community of 500 people may be incorporated as a village on application to the Provincial Government. The village may be raised to the dignity of a town when the population has reached the fifteen-hundred mark. The population qualification for a city is 10,000.

Village drunk. (See Drunk).

Virginia fence, a zig-zag rail fence.

Vote. A British subject qualifies for voting at elections after one year's residence in Canada, and a foreign subject after naturalization at the end of three years' residence. (See Naturalization).

Voyageur, a Canadian boatman or canoeist; one of the hardy race of men who made long voyages up the rivers to distant posts and returned with their boats or canoes laden with skins and pelts for the fur merchants of Montreal. So impressed was Lord Wolseley (then Colonel) with the skill of the Canadian voyageur during the Red River expedition, that he transported a corps of them to Egypt to assist his 1884-5 expedition up the Nile.

W

Wad. (See Roll and Tightwad).

Wallaby, a coat made of wallaby fur.

Wampum, an Indian's belt, usually highly ornamented with beads or shells.

Wander-lust, the irresistible impulse to keep on the move and see as much of the Dominion (or the world) as possible in life's brief span; sometimes due to the call of the wild. There are many men in the West afflicted with this disease. They usually can adapt themselves to any old job, but only hold it down long enough to earn the money which will carry them on to the next city on which they have cast longing eyes.

Wanigan, a shallow river boat on which lumbermen are housed, getting their food on another wanigan, known as the **cook wanigan.**

Wapiti, the name by which the elk, or moose-deer, is known to the Indians.

War-bag, a cowboy's kit-bag; a word imported into the Canadian West from the ranch lands of the Western States.

War-paint, the extra special adornments of the Indians when on the warpath.

Warpath. When the Indians dug up the hatchet and sallied forth to seek the scalps of their enemies, they were said to be on the **warpath.**

Wash-out, a chasm or channel formed by the rushing of water, or a portion of the railway track which has been carried away by a flood. The newcomer may happen to make his first acquaintance with a **wash-out** when his train is "held up" by one on his westward journey.

Watch my smoke, watch me hustle, or watch the dust at my heels, as the young man boastingly said when he went West, determined to make his fortune. Indians surmise what is going on inside a teepee by the smoke issuing from the top of it; and, in their warfaring days, smoke from fires lighted on the hilltops was their method of signalling.

Water wagon. When a person has become teetotal, or cut out the drink, he is said to be on the **water wagon.** But there's a mighty splash when they fall off.

Watered stock, fictitious capital in a company or corporation. "But your stock is watered," protested the prospective shareholder. "I know it is," admitted the promoter of the new distillery corporation. "We had to water it to propitiate the temperance people."

'Way back, the favourite fashion of indicating some indefinite period of the "early days," when the precise date is forgotten or of no consequence—the days when the old-timer found no idle moments to write up his diary and when the increasing volume of his possessions had not yet called for the services of a private secretary.

Web-foot State, Oregon.

Well-drill, a machine for boring into the ground in search of water. Settlers in the West who have not a visible supply of water, are accommodated with the use of a well-drill by their Provincial Government.

Where do I get off at? (with the emphasis on the **"I"**), an exclamation synonymous with the Old-Country question, "Where do I come in?" and usually meaning "What about my share of the plunder?" or "Am I not to be recognized in this arrangement?" **"Where do you get off at?"** (with the emphasis on the **"you"**) may be the solicitous inquiry of the Westerner when he gives you a "red-hot shot," or when he is anxious to hear if you can cap his story with one better.

Well-in, well-off, well-to-do; also familiar or in close friendship with a person.

West (The), as generally understood, is that half of Canada stretching from Winnipeg, the Gateway of the Golden West, to the shores of British Columbia. To be perfectly precise, however, it might be stated here that **the West** begins at the eastern gable of the office of the "Western Canadian Dictionary," 56 Adelaide street, Winnipeg, (which by courtesy and some proprietorial right which we have not hitherto questioned, is called the office of the "Telegram" Job Printers, Limited), and ends at the three-mile limit in the Pacific Ocean.

Wet, the condition of a town which has successfully opposed the Prohibition Law and where drink is still sold. (See **Dry**.)

Whale, beat, thrash; usually used in reference to half-killing a man or a crowd. **Whaling,** a thrashing, a severe beating.

Whaler. (See **Sundowner**).

What do you know? a common salutation meaning "Anything new?" or "What news?" **What do you know about that?** what do you think of that? After displaying a piece of work or some article, or after relating some adventure, a Canadian will say, "What do you know about that? It is, however, merely an exclamation, and not an inquiry.

Wheat belt, the plains of Manitoba, Saskatchewan, and Alberta, the great wheat-growing portion of Canada.

Wheeler, a horse driven in shafts, or next to the wheels; **off-wheeler,** a horse driven on the right-hand side; **near-wheeler,** the horse on the left-hand side.

Wheels in his head is said in reference to a man of weak intellect or whose head is full of hallucinations.

Whiskers, a jocular salutation, as Hello, **Whiskers!**

Whiskey-soak, a heavy drinker.

White, straight, honest. **He's white** signifies that the person referred to may be trusted as a brother. **He's white all over** is a still more emphatic assertion of the person's genuineness. **He treated us white** is how reference might be made to dealings with such a person.

White House, the official residence of the President of the United States, at Washington, so called from its colour. It is officially known, however, as the Executive Mansion.

Wholesaler, the person who handles the manufacturers' goods, and sells them to the retailers.

Whopper, anything very large, fine, good; also a big lie.

Wick-i-up, a roughly-constructed Indian hut; an Indian's wigwam, or teepee.

Wiggle (verb), get busy, or get a hustle on. When a Western employer is handling a "rush" order, he may exhort his men to **get a wiggle on.**

Wigwam, an Indian's habitation, usually a tent.

Wild and Woolly West, that portion of the North American Continent lying beyond the pale of supercivilization, ancient conventionalities, and biled shirts. An Eastern writer long ago gave it this name, and apt alliteration's artful aid has made it stick.

Wild (The), a poetic reference to the trackless forest and the howling wilderness, a region that gives promise of peril and adventure, where nothing under the rank of a savage she-bear may be encountered. **Lure of the wild,** another phrase of poetic origin, and having reference to a disease much affected by sentimental newcomers with a big roll of dollar bills. Reduced circumstances and necessity for work is the common cure.

Wild-cat, reckless, hazardous. A Michigan bank which collapsed had a panther, or wild-cat, engraved on its notes, and banking institutions of an unsound character were afterwards known as wild-cat investments.

Wildcatter, a promoter of wild-cat schemes, a company promoter notorious for the risky nature of his "propositions."

Wild farm, a farm where cultivation has not been begun and where no houses have been erected. (See **Improved farm**).

Windbreak, a cluster of trees or other growths set up to shelter farms or dwellings from the tempest.

Windrow, a row of hay set up loosely to permit of quick drying.

Windshakes, cracks separating the concentric layers of wood from each other. Timber with this defect is called "shakey."

Winnipeg, the capital of Manitoba and the commercial metropolis of Western Canada. A short distance north of Fort Garry, the trading post and settlers' depot at the junction of the Red River and the Assiniboine, the first house on the plain was erected about the year 1860, and to the hamlet rising there was given the name of the great Manitoban lake, viz., Winnipeg, a name derived from the Cree Indian words, **Win,** murky, and **niply,** water, referring to the contrast between its water and that of the transparent lakes to the east. For ten years the hamlet grew, though very slowly, since it was more than four hundred miles from St. Paul, the nearest town in Minnesota to the south. In 1870, the first census of Winnipeg was taken, and showed 213 persons in the village. Eleven years afterwards, in 1881, there were 7985 people, and Winnipeg had been an incorporated city since 1874. In 1891, the population was 27,068, and in 1901 it had grown to 44,778. During the five succeeding years, the city practically doubled its population, and it has proceeded at the same rate ever since, though the manner in which the 1911 census was taken does not permit of any very accurate estimate.

Wire-pulling, secret influence or intrigue, more especially in political circles.

Wise, as frequently uttered in Canada, may be interpreted as "knowing," "has his weather eye open," or "knows all about it." **Getting wise** implies that a person is beginning to find things out, that he is tumbling to the meaning of things, or that he is beginning to see through a trick or a swindle. He may then say that he has **got wise** or has been **put wise,** in which latter case he may have **got wise** by experience or been **put wise** by a friendly counsellor.

Wise guy, a common term used in reference to the individual who credits himself with the possession of superior wisdom, but who may be expected to be outmatched every time. The **wise guy,** for example, has fixed his mind on getting a particularly desirable quarter section for a homestead, and is at the Land Office "bright and early," but a **wiser guy** (who, it is to be supposed, does not credit himself with extraordinary acumen) has been there and snapped it up before him.

Wolverines, people from the State of Michigan.

Won out, the expression to indicate a win, as "the local man **won out** in all events he entered for." The Old-Country way of expressing it, except that the Canadian adds the word "out."

Working his mouth, talking much and saying little.

Workhouse. None in Western Canada. (See **Pauper**).

Wreck, the word to apply to a railway accident; or, more correctly, **train wreck.**

Write-up, a descriptive newspaper report, or an advertisement in the embellished form of an article, and paid for as a reader. (See **Reader**).

Written, effected, completed. The word is used in this sense in insurance circles, as: "Insurance was written on it to the amount of $500."

Y

Yah (spoken with a drawl) and **Yep** (uttered sharply), are words meaning **Yes.**

Yahoo, a lout from the back-country, an ignoramus, a know-nothing.

Yankee, a native of the United States; more correctly, a citizen of that portion of the States known as New England.

Yankee-Doodle, a popular melody of the United States; said, however, to be of English origin.

Yapp, to talk without ceasing; or, as they would say in the Old-Country, to **jaw.**

Yarn, a story or narrative spun out to beguile the time, as on board ship. The word is, however, not very frequently heard in Canada, Westerners having several words of similar meaning which "go one better" in expressiveness.

Yeggman, a thieving tramp, a burglar.

Yell, a distinctive college chorus, which sounds particularly fierce when a company of the students have monopolized the centre seats of some small meeting or showplace.

Yep, yes. (See **Yah**).

Yiddish, the composite language of the Jews as spoken in Canada, Great Britain, and elsewhere. It is mainly Hebrew, but all the languages of Central Europe help in its construction.

You bet, certainly, to be sure, you may depend on it. (See **Bet**).

You don't say, another exclamation of surprise—usually feminine.

You have me beat. (See **Search me**).

You're the doctor, It's for you to say, or It's for you to prescribe. A cowboy who had given cause of offence to a pard remarked, "If you want to fight about it, all right; **you're the doctor.**"

Z

Zebra, a person of undiscoverable nationality. The haphazard student of ethnology in the Western camps divides mankind up into white men, red men, yellow men, greasers and niggers, but a **zebra** is "neither one nor the other, nor which." It is conjectured that he is striped, or has a streak of white, red, yellow and black.

Zero, a cipher, nothing, the neutral point from which a thermometer is graduated. The zero mark in the balance column of your bankbook means that you've got to get a hustle on and get once more on the ascending scale.

The Student of "English as she is spoke" in the Golden West must now wait patiently for the issue of a third enlarged edition, beguiling the time by getting better acquainted with the editor and mailing copies of this present edition to friends in the Old-Country who want to know about Canada.

72441